Princess

You Know Who You Are

Princess

YOU KNOW WHO YOU ARE

Francesca Castagnoli

ILLUSTRATIONS BY IZAK

BROADWAY BOOKS

NEW YORK

PRINTED IN THE UNITED STATES OF AMERICA

BROADWAY BOOKS and its logo, a letter B bisected on the diagonal,
are trademarks of Random House, Inc.

Visit our website at www.broadwaybooks.com

Visit the author's website at www.princessyouknowwhoyouare.com

First edition published 2003

Book design by Judith Stagnitto Abbate / Abbate Design
Based on a design concept by Terry Karydes
Illustrations by Izak—represented by Traffic N.Y.C.

Library of Congress Cataloging-in-Publication Data
Castagnoli, Francesca.
Princess : you know who you are / Francesca Castagnoli ; illustrations by
Izak. — 1st ed.
p.   cm.
1. Women—Humor.   I. Title.
PN6231.W6 C37 2003
818'.5407—dc21
2002038359

ISBN 0-7679-1052-4

1   3   5   7   9   10   8   6   4   2

For Mom and Dad,
who made me the princess I am;
and for David,
who always treats me like one.

Contents

Part Three: Your Reign

Reality is a world as you feel it to be . . .

as you wish it into being.

DIANA VREELAND

Princess

YOU KNOW WHO YOU ARE

Introduction

ONCE UPON A TIME becoming a princess took a
lot of sacrifice. Just ask Sleeping Beauty, Cinderella,
and Snow White. They had to battle evil stepmothers,
suffer poisoned fruit, and wait for Prince Charming to
rescue them. These days, given the popularity of tiaras,
lunch-hour facials, and the proliferation of high-
quality knockoffs, women are writing their own fairy
tales. When real royalty is behaving badly, uptown girls
are slumming it downtown, and your ex-boyfriend is
minting his first million, it's time for self-proclaimed
princesses to make their debut. Now you, your step-
mother, and women ice hockey players everywhere can
return to work with freshly painted nails and the telltale
splotches of a cold blue waxing—even on a Monday . . .
and before lunch. Why? Because more and more
women have discovered that the real road to enlighten-
ment begins with entitlement.

It sounds obvious now, but it wasn't always so. My personal journey to princesshood began in the early nineties when I was living in San Francisco and grunge was at its grungiest. Everywhere I went there'd be girls dressed in flannel shirts, torn jeans, and boots. They didn't look like lumberjacks; they looked cool. I was both impressed and envious of their orchestrated ease. So I tried it. I bought a flannel shirt and I clomped around in Doc Martens, but I didn't feel alternative; I felt like a burly foreman. As I donated my "vintage" finds back to Goodwill, I realized that while everyone else was tattooing their necks, rummaging through thrift-store bins for B.O.-free sundresses, and coloring their hair with shoe polish, the most badass thing I could do was get a French manicure.

Shortly after that I started a self-published magazine called *Princess*—with the tag line: You Know Who You Are. I took the label that was a stigma growing up on Long Island and so often associated with spoiled, helpless little girls in designer jeans, and turned it into my very own feminine-feminist movement, a personal lesson in entitlement therapy. I figured if everyone else could walk around like a rock star, why couldn't I be a princess— with all the kitten heels, custom lingerie, settees, and monogrammed cocktail napkins included. I produced my first issue and prepared to be ridiculed. Instead, I was inundated with hundreds of letters from women all over who also wanted to live the fairy tale.

I've stopped publishing the zine, but I still believe that inside every woman, no matter how she describes her personal style, is an inner princess who wants to pamper herself silly in pursuit of what she thinks is beautiful. We're all entitled to the fantasy: the parties, the De Beers moments, and the sexy underpants. I know that my expectations are high, that I'm prone to hyperbole. And I also know that there are thousands of women out there who spent many Halloweens walking around their neighborhoods dressed as Cinderella or Princess Leia who, like me, wouldn't mind getting back to the ball. *Princess, You Know Who You Are* is your invitation.

PART ONE

Your Debut

Other women may be content with being

queen for a day, but when you're

a princess, you're one for a lifetime.

ONE

Princess, You Know Who You Are...

or Do You?

IT'S NO SECRET that princesses have very definite ideas about what makes us happy, from the setting of our engagement ring to our choice of lighting in our office. Trouble is, sometimes our lives don't match our fairy tale. This book will help you discover if you're a true princess or just a royal pain in the ass. You'll be able to wake up each day knowing exactly what's expected of you and how to pull it off with the grace of Princess Grace. Consider it your coming-out party, your debut. *Princess, You Know Who You Are* is the book for you, the girl who expects everything (even if you don't always really expect to get it).

Let's get started by finding out just how much of a princess you are. Don't worry if your Princess Quotient is low; this book will bring your PQ right up where it belongs, to the level of Catherine Deneuve's, Diana Ross's, and J. Lo's. Please take out a pen* and take the PSAT (Princess Self-Assessment Test).

---

*If your pen is an Elsa Peretti, you can skip the test and go directly to "If I Can Lift My Hand It's Not Big Enough" Princess, page 9.

are you a princess or a royal pain in the ass?

Choose one answer to each of the following:

1. When shopping, I...

a. realize my wallet has more ATM receipts than dollars
b. break something and hide it in the display
c. unintentionally choose the most expensive item in the store

2. When somebody says they have good news, I...

a. clap excitedly
b. feel jealous
c. think for a split second that it's going to be about me

3. I'll get a waxing right before...

a. hell freezes over
b. a tropical vacation
c. foreplay

4. I can double my age to find...

a. how many men I've slept with
b. how many pairs of shoes I have
c. how many pairs of cubic zirconia studs I've lost and replaced

5. My boyfriend is annoyed by...

a. how long I talk on the telephone with my mother
b. how long I monopolize the bathroom
c. how long it takes me to say good-bye at a party
d. all of the above

6. I'm usually late for...

a. work
b. dates
c. parties thrown in my honor

7. I cut calories by...

a. signing up with Weight Watchers
b. sleeping through breakfast
c. eating only the frosting on a cupcake

8. I have given a holiday gift to...

a. an ex-boyfriend
b. my boss
c. my therapist, psychic, dry cleaner, masseuse, manicurist, trainer, hairdresser, doorman, bus driver, healer, and personal shopper (although she picked hers out herself)

9. I'm always forgetting...

a. my downstairs neighbor's name
b. what day it is
c. that I'm not famous

10. Bonus Question: I've worn a tiara...

a. on Halloween
b. at my wedding
c. while vacuuming

SCORING

The correct answer to all the questions above is c, **except** for number 5, which is d. (Remember, in the world of princess there are always going to be exceptions.) But if we are going to get technical, for every question you answered a give yourself one point, for every b give yourself two points, and for every c give yourself three points, and for that special d give yourself four points.

👑 (1 TO 10 POINTS)
HALF-CARAT PRINCESS

Being able to jump out of bed and leave the house with a wet ponytail and a fresh layer of lip balm in seven minutes or less is impressive. But did you know that some women have their most profound creative/spiritual/intellectual breakthroughs while applying concealer in the morning? We princesses like to call it "Zen and the Art of Self-Indulgence." Okay, Suzy Chapstick, it's time to take off those skis, combine your score with a friend's, and make your first appointment for a mani/pedi where you'll ponder the complexities of merlot versus bordeaux nail polish.

👑 👑 (11 TO 20 POINTS)
ONE- TO TWO-CARAT PRINCESS

8

You'll need to be on a divan to hear this: You could be living so much larger. Sure, you play the part—you cut work for a sample sale and enjoy buying cocktail napkins. But just when you are about to fully embrace your inner princess with an act of wicked indulgence, like, say, hiring a feng shui consultant for your 400-square-foot apartment, something stops you short. What's haunting you? Insecurity? Laziness? FarmAid? What could be more worthwhile than yourself? Don't fear the pink, embrace it! Now go buy two pairs of strappy, sexy, practice-walking-in-your-panties sandals, have an orgasm, and call us in the morning.

👑👑👑 (21 TO 30 POINTS) "IF I CAN LIFT MY HAND IT'S NOT BIG ENOUGH" PRINCESS

Welcome, your highness. You remain unrecognized by the Queen of England, aristocracy, and the media, but who cares! You're hereby officially initiated into the special society of princesses who are the proud owners of at least one T-shirt that says "Hello, my name is Princess" and/or an apron that says "What do Princesses make for dinner? Reservations." Add your ability to rationalize buying a super-cute tankini after Labor Day, and you have proof that you do, indeed, know who you are. But you still need this book. Why? Just ask yourself this little question (which I'm sure you already know by heart): Is having it all ever really enough?

Identifying Characteristics

Unlike the Japanese club kids and Trekkies, you can't always spot a princess at ten paces. We do, however, have a few distinguishing characteristics that allow other princesses and perceptive admirers to notice us in any setting.

Perfectionism: Having grown up with a mother, sister, or gay uncle who aggressively, though lovingly, inspected you for flaws and was forever suggesting "cute" hairstyles, mole removal, nasal reconstruction, and weight loss, you strive for perfection in yourself and are conditioned to seek out the tiniest flaws everywhere.

Presentation: As the saying goes, princesses know "it's better to be looked over than overlooked," which is why the once-over is actually the princess version of a secret handshake.

Cuteness: The princess common denominator. Princesses use the word cute* to describe everything: feelings, innuendo, real estate, men, diamonds, stocks, salads...

Quality: Princess math determines that one four-ply cashmere sweater is greater than four one-ply cashmere sweaters.

Charm: You'll need to get on that salesman's good side if you want him to hold those perfectly slimming pants until they go on sale before charging and sending them to you.

*CUTE TRANSLATOR

"That's *so* cute": I've got to have that before anyone else.

"*Sooo cuuute*": Usually a response to something romantic tinged with jealousy, unless used to describe a man, infant, or animal.

"*That's* cute": Charge and send please.

"That's *cute*": That's cuter, so please charge and send this one instead of that one.

"Cute, Cute, Cute!!!": Invokes all of the above.

"*Cute*": I'm interested.

"Cu*te*": I told you so!

"Super cute": Absolutely.

"It's super cute": Thank you.

"Cute-iful": Describes someone or something that is much more cute than beautiful.

"Such a cutie": He's really sweet, and if he didn't have some real or perceived flaw (hair on his back instead of his head, love handles, or a serious girlfriend), you'd have sex with him.

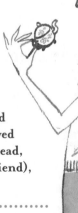

Generosity: You love to shop for your friends, never arrive at a party empty-handed, and, when in doubt, overtip.

Tact: You consciously refrain from turning the conversation to the tragedy of anorexia when your ex introduces you to his new girlfriend—who happens to be a model named Anka.

Attention to detail: The typeface for your wedding invitations, the slight discoloration above your lip that's developed after fifteen years of waxing, lingerie straps, quilted toilet paper, eggshell vs. ivory...

A continental attitude about cleanliness: Princesses suffer from the standard cleanliness clichés: you tidy for the cleaning woman, make sure the bathroom is spotless for Mom, and pretend to be French on weekends by refusing to shower and shave—until you have to get dressed for all those parties you're invited to.

A sense of destiny: Throughout your life you've secretly known you were meant for fame, fortune, and your very own walk-in cedar closet.

Entitlement: Comes in many forms: a room with a view, custom tailoring, more lemon in your Diet Coke; and since your dad and boyfriend think you always deserve special treatment, it comes as a small shock when meter maids, jury duty officers, and the IRS do not.

Princess Challenge

Study the Princess GRE (General Rules of Entitlement)
outlined opposite, then indulge in these practice tests.

Daily:

gym, orgasm (mechanically induced or otherwise),
meditation, champagne, dessert

Weekly:

breakfast in bed, aromatherapy, mani/pedi, shopping, tantrum

Monthly:

weekend getaway, spa treatment, workout in bed

Princess workout in bed:

Do ten leg lifts. Have sex. Rotate each leg in mini circles.
Have sex again. Do twenty mini leg lifts (only lowering the
leg halfway). Eat homemade breakfast in bed delivered to you
by darling boyfriend. Watch aerobically inspiring movie
(like Flashdance*). If he can keep up with you, have sex again.*
Rinse, repeat.

TWO

The Making of a Princess

Little princesses should be seen and heard.

MYTH:
Princesses are simply grown
spoiled children.

REALITY:
Being a princess is a choice
to live one's life the way it was fully intended.

THERE ARE MILLIONS of princesses in the world, but no two princesses are alike, even when they're wearing the same designer skirt. For instance, there's the jewelry princess who likes to buy her own diamonds, there's the triathlon princess who has each pair of sneakers custom-designed, the literary princess who quits her job every summer to attend a writers' colony, and the closet princess who doesn't even think she's a princess except for the fact that she orders fresh-squeezed orange juice and asks the waiter to strain the seeds, covers all bathroom door handles with a napkin after she's washed her hands, and only flies if she can have bulkhead seats. So what do all these individually fabulous women have in common? They each feel uniquely entitled to live their lives according to their own master plan. But how did they reach this enlightened state? Was it luck? A heavy influence of Madonna? Research suggests that it's their mother's fault.

To truly understand your princess roots you must first ask yourself: Am I my mother's daughter? Your mother's Princess Quotient is the key to your true princess nature. Her attitude unlocks the keys to your contradictions and quirks. Once you discover what kind of princess *she* is, you'll develop a deeper understanding of your own inborn aversion to wire hangers, why you shop for cocktail party supplies at Price Club, and your need to serve condiments in small, cute dishes.

Note: Fathers do not affect your Princess Quotient because every girl is her daddy's little princess.

····· QUIZ: ···

As a child you most remember your mother...

a. curling her eyelashes while driving

b. waking you up Saturday mornings by vacuuming outside your bedroom door

c. coaching your brother's little league

If you said *a,* your mother is a Glam-mama-zon and you are a legacy princess.

If you said *b,* your mother is a June Cleaver Overachiever, and you are a perfectionist princess.

If you said *c,* your mom is an antiprincess, and you are pioneer princess.

The one question that you heard your whole life was "That's your mother?!" She was the talk of the PTA with her whiskey voice, fluffy hair, and that fur coat she wore to the supermarket. She'd help you get dressed for school by pulling up your tights and pinching your legs with her manicured nails, cigarette in mouth and smoke blowing through her nose—a ritual that introduced you to the notion of suffering for beauty. She loved surprising you—like the Christmas Eve she disguised herself as Santa Claus by putting depilatory cream on her brow, lip, and chin. You spent quality time together playing games like Help Mommy Get Ready to Go Out, which involved carefully putting her cigarettes

19

in her cigarette case. You understood that "Try this on" in glam-mama-zon means "I love you." Which is why, after a long day shopping together, you didn't really complain when she called you into her room to change the channel on her TV, like a human remote control. She tried to do the kinds of things more traditional mothers did, but they never felt quite right, like your tenth birthday when she bought a piñata but didn't know she was supposed to stuff it (and resorted to throwing lollipops from the back of the room when it cracked open and nothing fell out). To some, her discipline was erratic: You were allowed to drink champagne at age twelve but were never allowed to sit in her redecorated living room. Today, you travel to spas together, though she refuses to do anything that requires her to sweat—other than a steam bath. And she still surprises you, like arriving unannounced at your office right after her collagen treatment to treat you to lunch, partly because she needs you to make sure she won't dribble on her blouse.

You are a legacy princess: With the legacy rising sign, it doesn't matter if you decide to follow in your mother's stilettoed footsteps or follow Grateful Dead cover bands, princess is in your blood. Which means that if you're a hippie, you'll wear the rarest form of patchouli. If you're a bohemian, you'll collect only first-edition French paperbacks sans mildew. Even if you're a nun, you'll join the convent with the chicest habits. There's no escaping it.

Your fatal flaw: Laziness. Just because your mother is leaving you her jewelry doesn't mean you'll automatically inherit her style.

Your mission: First, realize that it's all just a matter of time before we become our mothers—there's no reason to be afraid. As a legacy princess you may want to carry on her tradition of supermarket chic, but refuse to age in the way she did, complaining about everything from her thighs to her eyes. Instead, you identify your most prominent flaw, find the magician to rid you of it— faster and more painlessly than she ever did—and share your triumph with her. That's what glam-mama-zons and their legacy princesses call progress.

THE JUNE CLEAVER OVERACHIEVER

Your mother put her education and/or career on the back burner to major in motherhood with minors in handcrafts and vacuuming. Her talents included tying perfect bows on pigtails and presents, training the dog to walk around the living room carpet not on it, crocheting bikinis, becoming the tennis club champion (women's division), sewing your clothes from *Vogue* patterns, baking everything from scratch, spitting on napkins to wipe your face, keeping such a clean house you could eat off her kitchen floor—not that she'd ever let you—and holding the world's record for not having sat down since 1976.

Her taste can be described as Ann-Taylored but doesn't exclude wearing funky jewelry from the Southwest. She never showed you how to apply mascara because she just wore a dab of lipstick, but she did teach you how to accept a compliment graciously and how to write sincere thank-you notes. She always seemed so

self-sufficient, but looking back you now recognize her cries for help, like when she started to freeze your bologna sandwiches and let them defrost in your lunch box to save time. And there was her habit of preparing in the extreme: wrapping holiday gifts in July, setting the table for a dinner party a week beforehand, and occasionally wrapping all the living room knickknacks in Saran Wrap so they wouldn't get dusty, and tragically forgetting to unwrap them before guests arrived. Shortly after these events, she got her real estate license and was the top-selling agent in the tristate area from 1986 until 1993, when she quit to become a full-time dog trainer.

You have a guilty-conscience rising sign: **On your way to** the seven A.M. meeting with Tokyo investors, you find yourself fantasizing about having time to do house-work, cook, and stay home to have children. Like your mother, you are an overachiever, but while she baked her own bread, you tell your clients how to spend theirs. Also like Mom, you rely on other people to make you happy, but while she expected you, your siblings, and your dad to satisfy her needs, you call on your masseuse, housekeeper, and Señor Vibrator. You know your mom worries that you work too hard and will never get married. In her mind, girls today just have too many choices. But you also know that she's just a tiny bit jealous of your lifestyle. So on those rare days when you're not in a total crunch, you do feel a tinge of guilt about hiring a cleaning woman for your studio apartment, spending "that kind of money" to get your hair colored, slinking home after a night out with Mr. Hot Tub, expensing all those dinners, and relaxing with ritual paraffin treatments. Luckily you order a cham-pagne cocktail and snap out of it.

Your fatal flaw: **Surrender. There will be days when you** ask yourself why you're so damned picky, and wonder if everything would be fine if only you could get married and give her a grandchild. Remember, that fantasy is an illusion: It's like believing that Martha Stewart ever used her own brand of house paint and bath towels from Kmart.

Your mission: **Continue to serve yourself large doses of** personal happiness, but cut back on the bittersweet "guilt" flavoring. Your indulgences are part of your independence. You shouldn't feel obligated to work a seventy-hour week before you can call in a single measly mental health day. Don't worry if you're too busy to deal with these issues; they'll go away with time. But why wait? Go to a healer who will rid you of the guilt in your crown chakra, or schedule more time with harried girlfriends who've just had their first baby and haven't slept in weeks so that you can create a new fantasy, complete with nanny and housekeeper.

THE ANTIPRINCESS

There are as many antiprincess mothers as there are toy breeds of dogs. Your mom may have been a hippie known for having unshaven legs underneath her batik skirts and making "healthy" Easter baskets filled with Japanese seaweed, sesame candy, carob eggs, and sunflower seeds—a gift that killed the Easter bunny for you. She may have been a serious academic who was much more keen on teaching you Plato, Borgia, and Dickinson than how to bleach your upper lip. She could have been a weathered sportswoman—a sailor, rider, runner, fisherwoman who accessorized her slickers, jodhpurs, and track pants with a cooler. Or maybe she was a corporate lawyer in suits and sneakers who'd comfort you with the chicken soup she bought from the gourmet deli around the corner from her office. No matter who she was, one thing was for sure: Sometimes you thought it would have been easier on her if you were a boy. Your mom just didn't have the fuss gene, and the girlier you became the less she knew what to do with you. Especially on those Saturdays when you begged her to take you shopping but she was too "busy" organizing peace rallies, captaining crews, or filing last-minute motions to the federal court to take you to the mall—but you suspected it was really because she didn't have the faintest idea where it was.

You are a princess pioneer: Like the many self-made princesses who've come before you: Joan Baez, Cher, and Jewel. It's possible that your attraction to all things princess started out as a typical teenage rebellion: You asked for a faux-fur coat when you were thirteen, and begged to go hiking at Camp Beverly Hills just to spite

her. But over the years you realized that it wasn't an act—you really did feel more at home on the sterling silver floor of Tiffany & Co. than in a moldy tent.

Your fatal flaw: Believing you can't be a princess unless you're born to it.

Your mission: Realize that as a first-generation princess you have a huge advantage—without a mother to compete with on any princess level, you will always measure up. You are blessed with a collapsible sense of entitlement. You are capable of hiking for miles in the steamy, stinky Costa Rican rain forest without uttering a single complaint, but can also shift into high princess gear when pregnant and refuse to take public transportation. In addition, you get to make your own traditions, mantras, and rituals to be followed for generations to come—all because you had your first blow-out in the seventh grade.

The Princess Education

LANGUAGE

Princesses are style savants. We knew, at a very early age, how to spell, pronounce, and punctuate certain words that eluded our fellow classmates. Entertain yourself and friends by becoming familiar with the Princess vocabulary list.

Arrondissement *(Ah-rawn-deez-mahn)*: French for neighborhood, your favorite is the sixth in Paris, otherwise known as the Rive Gauche. You consider it your home away from home even if you've never been there.

Barneys: a house of worship.

Beluga *(Bell-u-ga)*: a picnic staple.

Chic *(Sheek)*: advanced placement cuteness.

Feng shui *(Fun[g] shway)*: another reason to re-arrange your bedroom.

Foie gras *(Fwah-grah)*: the first of a two-appetizer dinner.

Hermès *(Er-mes)*: the shade of l'orange you have chosen for your office.

Huahine *(Who-wha-hay-ney-hee)*: your first honeymoon destination.

Liposuction *(Lie-po-suction)*: a facelift for your thighs.

Nevis *(Knee-vis)*: your second honeymoon.

Radicchio *(Rad-dick-e-oh)*: cute lettuce.

Sangfroid *(sang-fwa)*: keeping your head at a designer sample sale.

Veuve Clicquot *(Vu-[r]ve Klee-ko)*: bubbly.

Note: **This test fulfills the language requirement for future fashion editors.**

ARITHMETIC

While others were slaving over algebra, geometry, and calculus equations, we were busy developing our brand of princess math. Here are a few sample questions for you to try.

1. *Percentages:* A princess just got double highlights and single-process coloring for $126.50 with tax. How much should she tip her colorist? The colorist's assistant? The hair-washer and the coat-check woman?

For an extra 10 points: What would be different if the colorist owns the salon?

2. A princess is getting a pedicure. The diameter of each toenail ranges from less than three quarters of an inch (big toe) to one eighth (pinky). How long will princess have to wait until she can put on her pumps if the fan speed is set to medium?

3. If the cost of a sweater set is $98 without tax, but you charge and send it to your parents' summer house in New Jersey, how much is the total price?

ANSWERS

1. Tip your hair colorist 20 percent for a grand total of $25.30 Round up to $26, as you'll never squeeze those quarters into the back pocket of his leather pants. A 15 percent tip for the colorist's assistant is $18.98. Round up to $19. A 10 percent tip for the hair-washer is $12.65. Round up to $13. Coat check gets $1 for every $50 spent, give her $3 (why not) and a smile.

Bonus Question: Technically, you don't have to tip the owner of a salon. That said, a scant few, even at the toniest salons, consider accepting pudgy minienvelopes insulting. It comes down to one thing: Your colorist has your hair in his hands. Withhold at your own risk. If you don't feel comfortable tipping your stylist, call Jasmine at Neuhaus Chocolatier and ask her to put together the "Hairdresser" gift basket.

2. She never puts on her pumps. Princesses have pedi-protecting flip-flops for every season, including fur-lined flops for the winter months.

3. There is no sales tax on clothing in New Jersey. The cost of the sweater (without shipping) is $98.

29

Extracurricular Activities

Princesses didn't join after-school activities to become more well-rounded, we joined clubs to further our princessness.

Cute skirt activities: tennis, ballet, figure skating, golf, cheerleading, field hockey, and lacrosse (depending on school plaid)

Minimal bodily harm: playing the triangle

Hawaiian Tropic tanning opportunities: lifeguard

Large accessory activities: horses, sailing, gemology, art collecting, jet-setting

Proximity to cute boys: skateboarding, cheerleading, trying out for and joining the boys' soccer, track, and baseball teams

Proximity to cute boys who love to talk about clothes: drama

Present-making: jewelry, arts and crafts

Tantrum management: drums, modern dance, riflery

After-school Specials

What princesses learned through TV:

"Gilligan's Island": When in doubt, channel Mrs. Howell and overpack.

"Charlie's Angels": Your popularity is directly related to your hairstyle.

"The Facts of Life": Boarding school makes you fat.

"I Love Lucy": Funny ≥ Beautiful.

"Bewitched": Pug noses are powerful.

"I Dream of Jeannie": You can wear the same thing every day as long as it's fabulous.

"Mary Tyler Moore": You're gonna make it after all.

GREAT MOMENTS IN PRINCESS HISTORY

c. 605 B.C.E.: The hanging gardens of Babylon, the second wonder of the ancient world, are built for Queen Amuhia by her husband, Nebuchadnezzar.

c. 0: Mary of Nazareth gives birth to Jesus. Even though she delivers him in a manger among the lowing of the animals, it's a classy affair with foreign dignitaries arriving fashionably late with gifts.

1559: Queen Elizabeth I passes sumptuary legislation condemning excess in apparel that forbids her ladies-in-waiting to dress better than she does and also forbids others to wear the colors and styles that favor her. At one time she possesses more than eighty wigs, twenty-seven fans, and three thousand dresses.

1764: Madame de Pompadour, mistress of Louis XV, prepares to meet her maker. While the priest is giving her the last sacraments, she calls on God to "wait a second" and proceeds to apply two dabs of rouge to her cheeks.

1855: Lucy Stone becomes the first woman on record to keep her own name after marriage, setting a trend among women who are consequently known as "Lucy Stoners."

c. 1856: Empress Eugénie, wife of Emperor Napoléon III, has her ball gowns made in duplicate so that halfway through the evening she can change, then reappear looking fresh and dazzling.

c. 1910: Rita Lydig carries loose emeralds and sapphires in her pockets and gives them to the shop vendors in exchange for their help. Rumor has it that, when asked why, she answered, "What do you expect me to tip them with?"

1916: Margaret Sanger and her sister, Ethel Byrne, open the first U.S. birth control clinic in Brooklyn, New York.

1925: Before Gloria Swanson returns to the States from Paris with her new husband, the Marquis Le Bailly Henri de la Falaise de la Coudraye, she sends Cecil B. DeMille a wire noting, "Am arriving with the Marquis tomorrow. Stop. Please arrange an ovation."

1934: In the movie *Scarlet Empress,* Marlene Dietrich wears what is considered the world's largest mink muff.

1937: While working at *Harper's Bazaar,* Diana Vreeland complains that she can't hack the twelve-hour days at the office. A colleague politely suggests she break for lunch. Diana is thrilled by the idea.

1940s: Elizabeth Arden produces a white velvet gas mask.

c. 1940: Joan Crawford carries 100-proof vodka in hip flasks with specially designed covers that match her outfits. She also wears falsies so that when she lies down her breasts will point skyward.

c. 1950: Teenage Doris Duke's limousine is equipped with a panic button she could push whenever a boy tried to kiss her.

1966: After wearing two oversized necklaces—one ruby and one diamond—to Truman Capote's Black and White Ball, Gloria Guinness has to rest in bed all day.

1973: Billie Jean King scores an enormous victory for female athletes when she beats Bobby Riggs in "The Battle of the Sexes," a televised tennis tournament watched by nearly 48 million people.

1977: Doris Royal, a farm wife from Springfield, Nebraska, files with Congress 231,261 signatures from forty-nine states to fight outmoded estate tax laws that fail to recognize a woman's equitable status in joint tenancy should her husband's death precede her own.

1979: Unable to get her beloved Diet Coke in Europe, Christina Onassis sends her jet to America once a month for ten cases direct from the factory at a cost of $30,000, which includes the fuel and pilots' salaries, or $3,000 per case. Her soda pop palate becomes so evolved that she is able to tell if a can is more than one month old or, as in the case of regular Coke, in which European plant it was bottled.

1979: Debbie Shook smashes her Miss North Carolina crown when state Jaycees retract her title for her statement that being a beauty queen is not "a bed of roses."

c. 1980: Imelda Marcos has a bulletproof bra made.

1989: Leona Helmsley is sentenced to four years in prison for evading over $1 million in federal taxes. She served eighteen months and was assigned 750 hours of community service. In 1995, members of her domestic staff revealed that they had performed the court-ordered work for her.

1999: Jennifer Lopez is jailed with boyfriend Sean "Puffy" Combs after a shooting incident in a New York City nightclub. She allegedly asks a cop for cuticle cream while handcuffed.

2001: Catherine Deneuve's seemingly ageless face is rumored to be held up by a fine, subcutaneous web of 22K gold stitches.

Princess Challenge

Have lunch with your mother
without rolling your eyes at her during the entire meal.

PART TWO

Your Coronation

THREE

Princess Shopping

Shop unto others
as you would have them
shop unto you.

MYTH:
Princesses are shopaholics.
If that were the case, we'd all be home
watching QVC, collecting gold S-chains
and *Little Women* dolls.

REALITY:
Princesses shop because it's
the modern-day equivalent of a quilting circle.
We see friends, get the scoop,
and reflect on who we are.

My Fashion Muse

Shortly after Richard Burton had given Elizabeth Taylor the Krupp diamond—33.19 carats—she bumped into Princess Margaret and showed it to her. Princess Margaret said, rather haughtily, that it was the most vulgar thing she'd ever seen, but Elizabeth offered to let her try it on. "See," Elizabeth said as the princess was admiring it on her own finger, "it's not so vulgar after all."

I RECENTLY BECAME an Elizabethan. Not the Renaissance fair–medieval kind, the Hollywood kind. Elizabeth Taylor is my fashion muse. Cultivating a fashion muse is easy. You simply think of the style of someone you admire—a character in a film or book, or a real person—and shop with them in mind. My friend Ann has been doing it for years. She has a nice tough-but-tender rock-star thing going; when she shops she asks herself, in earnest, "Would Leather Tuscadero wear this?"

Finding your fashion muse is a princess rite of passage; it's a way of baptizing your style. Your muse helps you purify your closet by devoting it to the essence of who you'd like to be. The fashionable have been tapping into the fabulous for years. Sharon Stone had Marlene Dietrich, Madonna had Marilyn, and Gwyneth had Grace. Similarly, a princess turns to her muse to keep herself from going off on unflattering fashion tangents. And as we grow into our muse, we get a free gift with every purchase: a lesson in shopping discipline.

Flipping through a magazine, I noticed a photograph of Elizabeth Taylor and Richard Burton in Puerto Vallarta. Boatneck top, bright capris, hair swept back in a bouffant ponytail. Her clothes were preppy in the way resort clothes always are, but she wasn't stiff. There was an exuberance in her thick gold necklace with a large medallion, the jangle of her gold bracelets, and her smile. Her aura turned plain-old khaki into couture—she may have looked casual on the outside, but she was dressy on the inside. In that moment, my fashion muse crystallized.

Elizabeth loved to dress up on special occasions, and, being Liz Taylor, every day was an occasion. I'm infatuated with her fashion in both her movies and her reality—the full slip in *Butterfield 8,* the white chiffon dress with the plunging neckline in *Cat on a Hot Tin Roof,* mod poncho tops and hot pants in *X, Y, & Zee,* and her jewelry collection (roughly $23 million worth of ice).* What I admire most about Elizabeth's style is that she knew what to do with both her body and her jewels: show them off. Before Elizabeth, I thought I had style,

*According to a 1973 appraisal. Estimates now place her collection in the gazillions.

but the ugly truth was that I was defenseless against trends. *Vogue* demanded I do frayed denim miniskirts. Banana Republic loved stretch trousers in pink. Barneys advocated studded T-shirts. Even if these clothes were suspect, without Liz as my fashion compass, I still considered them. Now my wardrobe is divided into two categories: clothes B.E. (Before Elizabeth) and clothes A.E. (After Elizabeth). In my A.E. period, I shop with the missionary zeal of someone born again. When I see something cute I ask, "WWED?" ("What would Elizabeth do?"), and amazingly I'm able to waltz past racks of trendy clothes made for Twiggy, Marcia Brady, or Cyndi Lauper without looking back. I feel as complete as a set of monogrammed luggage.

Now that Liz and I have hit our stride, I've found a way to kick my fashion musing up a notch. It's my own fashion genome project: I fuse superstars with heiresses to create fashion-muse hybrids. All it takes is indulging in a little game of Six Degrees of Liz Taylor. Let's play: Liz Taylor was married to Nicky Hilton, who socialized with Babe Paley, an heiress who worked and often posed for Diana Vreeland's *Vogue*; Vreeland probably got a kick out of Studio 54, where Diana Ross would arrive in show-stopping hairstyles that looked just like what Liz Taylor wore in *Cleopatra*. Now, let's try on a few of these combinations: "Elizabeth Paley": blinding diamond rings (Taylor) and perfectly tailored capri pants and prim oxfords (Babe Paley). Or "Elizabeth Vreeland": low-cut chiffon-ish dress (Taylor) with chunky turquoise or jade jewelry and slicked-back hair (Diana Vreeland). Or "Elizabeth Ross": me drinking champagne (Taylor) and singing while wearing sequins (Diana Ross).

What Princesses Talk About When They Talk About Shopping

Black = Attitude. Princesses agree with Goths on one fashion point: Black is a state of mind—though we've been known to ask salesgirls for something darker.

Trends = Self-reflection. Even if we don't subscribe to, let's say, the return of fringed epaulets on shirt-dresses, every new fad allows us to indulge our favorite question: Is it me?

Sales = Freedom. A sale is the frozen yogurt of shopping; it lets us indulge without consequences.

Jewelry store windows = Ambition. Like moths to a flame we are magnetically drawn to windows displaying diamonds, rubies, sapphires. Jewelry stores encourage us to think big, as in carats.

Out of stock = Tragedy. Princesses expect a great deal out of life, and since shopping has its fair share of trauma, we sometimes find ourselves having a hard time handling loss—like when we finally find the perfect pants but the store doesn't have our size. Luckily, we're professionals who've evolved some tricks of the trade that less-seasoned shoppers don't have: a sense of risk and the five stages of shopper's grief.

SHOPPER'S RISK

See cute skirt in window. Try cute skirt on, realize they only have one left in your size, postpone purchasing item (for a good reason, like dog's bladder will burst). Go back next day and discover it's gone...

the five stages of shopper's grief

DENIAL:
"Wait, it *has* to be here. I tucked it behind a yellow size-fourteen sundress."

ANGER:
"I hate separates anyway!"

Note: **Spiritually advanced shoppers have been known to subscribe to what L.A.-based yogis call accessory reincarnation. Celebrities have reported missing shoes coming back as found earrings, or a stolen wallet leading to unexpected discounts at a favorite boutique. For these evolved creatures all loss is part of the karmic circle of shopping.**

46

BARGAINING:
"I promise that if you can special-order it for me, I'll buy three of them."

ACCEPTANCE:
"Maybe that skirt did make my butt look big?"

DEPRESSION:
"Everyone thinks I have no style. I deserve to spend the rest of my life skirtless."

The Joy of Shopping

Princesses prefer to shop with a friend. If we don't have a friend with us, we become friendly with the salesgirl. Some princesses admit to having a harder time finding the right shopping partner than finding their lifelong partner. But once we find that special pal, shopping can be as satisfying as sex: We both get what we want—and sometimes in multiples. With all this intensity associated with shopping, princesses wisely separate their relationships into two categories: friendships and friendshops.

Caution: Good friends can easily mistake their friendship for a friendshop and end up with bad feelings, and even worse purchases. So, be careful, and save time and money by committing to the Princess Friendshop Pledge.

• Princess Friendshop Pledge •

I Princess,

Will say yes to a shopping excursion nine times out of ten (even when I don't "need" a thing).

Will reveal my full shopping agenda in detail so that my friend and I can coordinate our strategies and make a unified attack.

Allow for the Princess Grace Period because I know that when a princess says she's leaving "now," it really means she's leaving in fifteen minutes—okay, twenty.

Won't get weird when my friend buys the same shirt because I know that (a) we have our own individual style, (b) we can call each other when we want to wear it if we'll be meeting up, and (c) imitation is the highest form of flattery.

Can carry on an intense conversation about my relationship/job/mother/ex while browsing and I am not offended if my friend cuts me off mid-sentence to point out a pair of super-cute shoes.

Possess an encyclopedic knowledge of my friend's wardrobe so I know what she's referring to when she says, "Would this (insert item) go with my cute top?"

Can help my friend rationalize any worthwhile extravagance by dividing the price by the number of times she'll wear it.*

Princess Signature   *Date*

---

*Excluding wedding dresses, which have a separate advisory counsel.

Wondering who your best shopping partner is? How can you know unless you shop together? This simple profile will help you take the mystery out of shopping with friends by providing you with common shopping profiles and clues you can look for before you sacrifice a day out in the field.

Note: These habits are not mutually exclusive. Over time (from an hour to a year) one princess can cycle through each of these moods depending on her schedule, workload, and recent tax refund.

The Scout: This highly motivated veteran can put in three to four hours of shopping a day without realizing it. She buys things at places where nonscout types wouldn't even know there's stuff for sale: aquariums, churches, the dermatologist. Can often be overheard saying "That would be great for..."

• *Tip-off:* When she gives directions, she doesn't use street names, only retail landmarks.

The Remote Shopper: A woman whose life is marked by busyness or who is a new media professional. The remote shopper prefers to shop on-line or through catalogs. When she calls local stores to have her purchases charged and sent, she returns them via company FedEx. Friends call her the Cliff Notes of Catalogs.

• *Tip-off:* Bedside reading—the complete works of Williams-Sonoma, Bliss, Neiman Marcus, and Anthropologie. Web pages are bookmarked by category: clothes, flatware, shoes, linen, and so on.

The Stalker: A regular customer though she rarely buys anything. The stalker visits one particular item (sometimes for weeks) and asks the price each time (though she knows it) as a symbolic act of shopping.

• *Tip-off:* Freely admits she had a habit of calling her seventh-grade crush and hanging up. Can still remember his number.

The Nibbler: The progressive shopper, she browses the store, buys one small thing, feels satisfied, comes back within seventy-two hours to buy something else. Repeats until full and or has bought everything that fits her figure and budget.

• *Tip-off:* Never takes a whole cookie off a plate. Instead, she breaks off small bites, piece by piece, until she's eaten the whole cookie—and in some cases one or two more.

The Free Spirit: Hasn't paid retail in seven years and considers being a member of Price Club a hobby. Has a closet filled with gifts (free with purchase or bought at discount stores) just in case someone suddenly needs a present.

• *Tip-off:* Is usually dating a couple of guys at once because she can never say no to anything that's two-for-one.

The Speedster: Can glance in a store and take in the entire inventory in seconds. Speedsters hold the world's record for getting out of the Mall of America in one hour and forty-six minutes.

- *Tip-off:* Is also a speed reader.

The Exchange Student: A regular customer who second-guesses her choices due to (1) the fear of overspending, (2) a look from her mother, or (3) the discovery of something cuter. Lax return policies have been known to turn Exchange Students into "Exchange Bingers" and then into "Nibblers" until they have used up their store credit.

- *Tip-off:* While ordering lunch she will change her order from a hamburger to a turkey club and back again only to later mention that she wishes she had ordered the turkey club.

A GREAT FIT: POPULAR FRIENDSHOPS

The Scout and the Stalker: Stalkers like to shop with scouts because they increase their stalking radius.

The Scout and the Free Spirit: During a sale, the Scout acts as the Free Spirit's shopping agent, pointing out things her cute-radar picked up days before, helping the Free Spirit find her size, snagging the roomiest dressing room, and knowing who to ask for in alterations.

The Stalker and the Free Spirit: Stalkers like to shop with Free Spirits so that they can marvel at how quickly and deftly Free Spirits can score so many amazing discounts in one day. Stalkers can also be stealth enablers caught in a duality of being thrilled by each purchase and yet relieved it's not their own cash being spent.

The Stalker and the Nibbler: These two can shop together as they both enjoy the tension of resisting, though Nibblers eventually break down and buy something small.

MOST COMMON FRIENDSHOP MISMATCHES

The Exchange Student and the Scout: An Exchange Student will occasionally ask an expert like a Scout for help. This pairing usually results in a complete makeover for the Exchange Student, which she then second-guesses and returns.

The Speedster and Any Other: Speedsters can only shop with other Speedsters, but even they tend to slow her down.

The States of Princess Shopping

Counter-Fit: The realization that your purchase is not worth putting up with (a) snobby sales staff, (b) holiday crowds, (c) perfume hawkers, or (d) all of the above.

Drive-Buy: See it. Love it. Charge it.

Indecision: All day you've told people what to do and how to do it, but for some reason you can't choose between the lilac or lemon skirt to save your life. Solution: Buy both.

Manic: Over-the-top extravagance even with a 70 percent discount. Usually occurs when you've just broken up with your boyfriend, started a new job, or it's January.

Zen: See the black suit. Try on the black suit. Become the black suit.

THE SHOPPING DIET

Bingeing: Marked by a decision to shop alone, bingeing is usually triggered by empty closet syndrome, a chemical imbalance in a princess's wardrobe brought on by the sweet yet panicked arrival of spring and a deficiency of opened-toe sandals.

Purging: Princesses periodically engage in a shopper's bulimia where we joyfully rid ourselves of the past year's experiments to make room for new a wardrobe.

The Elements of Princess Style

Princesses don't have to actually buy stuff to shop. In fact, there are days—lots of them—when we prefer to be consumer anthropologists working toward our M.W.S. (Masters in Window Shopping) degree. M.W.S. requirements are:

1. *Bionic vision:* We should be able to spy a cute tote in a store window from fifty meters.
2. *Stealth appraising:* We can guesstimate prices more accurately than the Keno brothers on "Antiques Roadshow."
3. *Style agility:* Although we don't agree with the idea of shopping as a competitive sport, princesses love to play a little game called Buy-or-Cry while window shopping. Each player surveys a store window—the tackier, the better—and the first to find something she'd actually buy wins.
4. *Completion* of 150 hours of window-shopping research work—usually completed in less than a week.

The Princess Wardrobe Pyramid

A Guide to a Well-Balanced Closet

Diamonds (in large blinding doses): rings, earrings, necklaces, bracelets, tiaras, scepters

The Second Skins Group (5 to 10 servings): leather, shearling, vintage snakeskin, lizard, alligator, crocodile, ostrich, fur, feathers, marabou

The Accessories Group (30 to 40 servings): handbags, clutches, totes, belts, jewels, train cases, fancy dog leashes

The Terry Group (5 servings):
slippers, robes, bikinis, loungewear, shower
curtains, dressing room table settees

The Lingerie Group (15 to 20 servings):
matching bras and panties, naughty
thongs, pretty negligees, demure white
cotton nighties

The Shoe Group
(20 to 200 servings):
stilettos, kitten heels,
mules, slides, sneakers,
boots, flip-flops,
slippers

Obsessive Closet Design (OCD)

Closet Mantra: "No matter how big the closet, it could always be bigger."

The No-No: Improvisation. It's eight A.M. Do you know where your outfit is? Yes. Princesses answer this troubling question by laying their clothes out the night before and/or waking up with a mental picture of what we plan to wear, which came to us in a dream.

The Enemy: Wire Hangers. Otherwise known as closet kryptonite, wire hangers weaken our style by allowing us to overstuff closets and leave indelible points in the shoulders of our blouses, making us wish for the return of shoulder pads. Exception: clothing sent out to the dry cleaner that stays in tissue/hanger/plastic while in storage.

The Weapon: Puffy Hangers.
One puffy hanger takes up
the space of three hangers
whose name we shall not
speak so they force
us to ask tough

questions like, are we really going to wear those feathered jeans again?

The Philosophy: Emancipation Frocklimation. The understanding that clothes should be treated based on how they make us feel, not on how much they cost. Once we've decided what we want to keep, we'll pamper that sort-of-rare and very romantic $5 vintage sweater from Goodwill with the same puffy hangers and tissue paper as that triple-digit suede backless cocktail dress we can't afford to dry-clean.

The Legacy. The vintage alligator bag inherited from your great-grandmother, your grandmother's fur stole, and your mom's hat box from a department store (Bonwit Teller circa 1968). *Note:* If you are a pioneer princess, all of these items can be purchased on eBay.

the pièce de résistance

Your shoe storage is the cornerstone of closet obsession. Match your shoe storage with the following methods to find out what it reveals about you.

a. Shoe bags and shoe trees

b. Original shoe boxes with Polaroids taped on the outside

c. The oven

d. Willy-nilly on the floor of your closet

e. Shoe closet with mechanical doors

If you said *a* you're a **purist.**
If you said *b* you're an **addict.**
If you said *c* you're **punk rock,** pressed for storage, or both.
If you said *d* you're a **bohemian.**
If you said *e* you aspire to be **Goldie Hawn in *Overboard.***

Princess Challenge

*Banish shopping shame. When you come home from shop-
ping, instead of doing the shopping bag shuffle (where you head
straight to the bathroom complaining that you've had to pee for
an hour and stash your shopping bags in the tub), arrive with
your shopping bags in full view and announce how much money
you saved by tallying all the items you resisted.*

FOUR

Princess Pampering

*Good things come to those
who give themselves good things.*

MYTH:

All princesses are pampered.

REALITY:

All princesses are pampered.

PRINCESSES ARE often accused of living a fantasy life. We want parties, Pulitzers, custom lingerie, and corner offices. But if you think we're going to lounge around on a toile divan and moan until Daddy or hubby drops it in our lap, think again. We know that no one will treat us as well as we treat ourselves. We are the heads of our single-pamperer households (all princesses are heads of single-pamperer households even if they're married) and that means repeating the princess oath after me: I am my own sugar mama.

The Princess Pampering Manifesto

There is a nasty virus spreading among women. Its symptoms appear as helplessness, competitiveness, envy, greed, icy glares, and snotty comments. The bitchy germs are being passed from friend to friend, boss to protégée, colleague to client. These are the false princesses, the lost girls who refuse to introduce their also-single friends to an available bachelor, even if they're not interested in him. Who wear the latest "it bag" like their heart on their sleeve. Who treat a trip to the powder room as a beauty contest, painfully aware that there's someone thinner, prettier, richer, and more successful freshening up at the sink next to them.

The true princess is born with an antibitch antibody—she's not looking for outside confirmation of her fabulousness; she has a pink fire that burns from within. Here is her manifesto.

Every occasion is a special occasion. Princesses understand that pampering is not a once-and-a-while dial-up connection to indulgence, but a hard-wired T1 line to self-fulfillment. It's 4:40 P.M. on Tuesday and you're getting a hot stone massage because...well, because you want to. Our body is a temple. That's why we take such good care of it and listen to the bells tolling for chocolate, naps, and sex. It's our way of making a donation to our favorite charity: us.

Save yourself first. The airline safety instruction to "Place the oxygen mask on yourself, and then on child passengers" must have been written by a princess. Princesses know that in order to help others we must first help ourselves. For example, imagine having a meeting scheduled *before* your waxing appointment. Can you really expect to deliver a winning presentation if you're worried that the client can see your chin hair?

Surprise yourself. We do this by quietly letting a desire sit in the back of our mind and then suddenly acting on it. The "wow" can be as simple as calling in sick to spend the day shopping or as elaborate as popping off to the hairdresser for a trim and coming home with thermal reconditioning instead.

Keep it real. Faux fur and eyelashes are one thing, but princesses don't fake orgasms or friendships.

Leave town. Princesses know that no one is ever rewarded for not taking a vacation. We relax out of town, and often. Once there, we indulge our Room Lust by changing our suite once, twice, ten times until it's exactly how we imagined—and a tad more.

Teach by example. As princesses, we will treat ourselves to diamond jewelry (cubic zirconia can do the trick), send ourselves flowers, and take spa vacations because we're worth it and also to let our loved ones know what kinds of things make us happy.

Say yes as often as possible. Princesses accept invitations, gifts, a glass of water, the after-dinner drink, a seat, a compliment, and an extra topcoat.

Say no as often as possible. Even princesses know that too much of a good thing can be a bad thing, not to mention a complete bore. This is why we send our boyfriend home after three nights of slumber parties, don't ask for thirds on the watermelon martinis, and refrain from exercising on holy days.

Get over it. Princesses get up in the morning, look in the mirror, and say, "I forgive you." Of course, we still get embarrassed if we do something stupid, like fart while playing doubles, fall off our stilettos and sprain an ankle, or forget the name of our new boyfriend when introducing him at a Christmas party. But we have perspective, it could be worse: It could have been televised.

Listen to your inner princess. The only person a princess expects complete honesty from is herself. We have a natural talent for always knowing exactly what we want, even if we don't know how to get it. We hone our self-honesty skills with mental exercises that channel our inner princess. We imagine exactly what we want for lunch, how we'd decorate our office in our fantasy country house, and the precise moves of our five-year plan for world domination. (Little princess secret: When a princess tells someone "I don't know," she's lying. We always know. Occasionally, we may not know how to phrase our needs yet. But if you give us twenty minutes, we will.)

The Princess Pampering Datebook

THE WHO, WHAT, WHERE, WHEN OF INDULGENCE

week at-a-glance

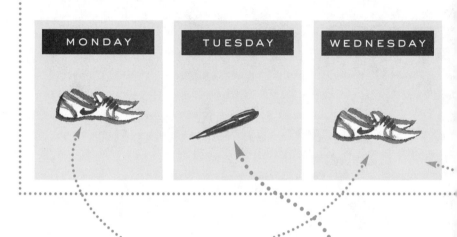

MONDAY   TUESDAY   WEDNESDAY

Your trainer:
Monday and Wednesdays
at 7:00 A.M.

Your therapist:
Tuesday at 3:30 P.M.

A princess doesn't look good if she doesn't *feel* good. So you make up for the Moët Chandon and two slices of flourless chocolate cake by subjecting yourself to ridiculously rigorous work-outs with a personal trainer/ex–Navy SEAL drill sergeant who is not only a hard-ass but has promised to give you a hard ass.

Having squandered your loved one's compassion reserves with statements like "I'm cranky," "I hate my clothes," and "My ankles are too thick," you've realized you need a "friend" to provide undivided, judgment-free attention each week. You're too impatient for analysis, but you do need sympathy, and lots of it.

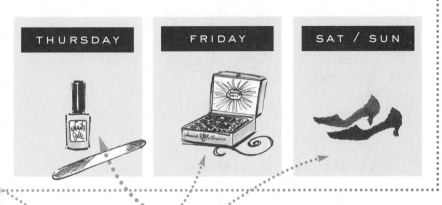

THURSDAY
FRIDAY
SAT / SUN

Your candy man:
Practically every day
at 4:00 P.M.

Visit this man's newsstand/
deli/frozen yogurt shop
to treat yourself to four
miniature peppermint
patties and a Diet Coke, or
a French vanilla and double
Dutch chocolate swirl with
sprinkles on top and
bottom.

Your manicurist/waxer:
Standing appointment
every Thursday at
6:30 P.M.

You treat your appointments
as a beauty confession:
"Forgive me, Anna, but I
have two hangnails, one
corn, and three chin hairs."
You repent promising her
son an internship while she
files your nails and and tears
off your facial hair, absolving
you of your beauty sins.

71

Your shoe salesman: As often as possible

When you walk in the door, he abandons whoever he's helping to whisper sweet nothings in your ear: "I saved you my last pair of slides in size eight." He has your card on file and calls you every time something cute arrives. Others may call him an enabler, but you call him family.

Your inner hippie: Weekends

After five days of hair, makeup, and uncomfortable shoes you allow your skanky alter ego to take over by spending Saturday or Sunday (or both) at home in your loungewear, unshowered, unshaved, and unself-conscious.

Your herbalist: Every two weeks

Tired of being dismissed by doctors as being "perfectly normal" despite headaches, upset stomach, and general fatigue, you've sought out an expert who actually wants to hear the details of all your aches and pains. Each night you faithfully drink the special herbs she mixed exclusively for you, swearing you'll never see another doctor again (unless one asks you out).

Your dermatologist: Every four or five months

Your derm isn't as much a doctor as your "youth consultant." Not only did she put you on the exact same beauty regimen as Ms. Universe, she was honest enough to say you don't need the glycolic freckle remover cream, or collagen, but you could use Botox for your furrowed brow. Since then, you feel four inches taller.

Your hairdresser: Every six weeks

The only person who knows you have gray. You worship her—you would have to decline an offer to relocate across the country unless she could come with you, because life without her is meaningless.

Your psychic: Every four months

Your happily-ever-after guarantee. She frequently foresees a cloudy but attractive future anchored by intriguing landmarks—a stone cottage...a blond rock climber...Provence—that gives you something to look forward to when in doubt.

Princess Beauty

Here are a few tiny ways to indulge yourself today.

- Make cookie dough, but forget to bake the cookies and just eat the dough
- Buy an exotic flower and wear it in your hair or as a pin
- Adopt a fluffy dog
- March out right now and finally buy yourself that chandelier you've been dreaming about. Hang it in your bathroom
- Get your own place and kiss roommates good-bye
- Sleep naked . . . alone
- Throw a party at a restaurant or bar so you don't have to clean up
- Custom-blend your own perfume
- Name your apartment or house
- Put crème de La Mer all over your body
- Wear large, sparkly cocktail rings during the day
- Put your cold eye-gel pack on your nipples
- Open a bottle of champagne when you only want one glass

JOIN THE WWF
(WORLD WAXING FEDERATION)

Are you a hair-removing heavyweight willing to endure brutal torture for smooth, stubble-free skin? If so, give yourself a nickname (Stache, The Bleacher, Tweeze, or Rip) and join the princess World Waxing Federation by signing the petition on the next page.

· Pain-free Hair Removal Petition ·

We, the undersigned members of the WWF, strongly believe that until a pain-free hair removal process is available and offered to the public (and at a reasonable price), beauty technicians should have mandatory anesthesiology training and licensing.

We do not agree that hair removal falls in the "no pain, no gain" category.

We believe that bathing suit manufacturers are putting our bodies at risk by encouraging us to suffer unnecessary torture and ingrown hairs.

We reserve the right to popularize bikini bathing suits for men so that all of mankind will feel pressured to manage their body hair the way women have for years. Once men experience the trauma of removing their hair, Congress will promptly redirect defense funds to invent a pain-free process, but for the sake of good taste we do not want to see men in bikini briefs before we have to resort to this.

Signature   Date

When Is It Too Much?

For some of us too much is never enough. If seeing a healer once makes all the pain go away, why not see her until you're numb? If B$_{12}$ shots energize us, why not have one every day instead of cappuccino? This is the world of pampering dangerously. Enter at your own risk.

THE SECRET MEANING OF PONYTAILS— A.K.A. OVERSLEEPERS ANONYMOUS

Are you a candidate for OA? Find out by checking which of the following statements applies to you. Beyond experiencing extreme difficulty removing yourself from your perfect cocoon of featherbed, eye mask, soothing whale lullabies, silk sheets, and organic down comforters, you...

1. Would sleep until the last hour of the "Today Show" without two alarm clocks.
2. Spend the majority of your commute flipping through your Rolodex of excuses: doctor's appointment; sick dog;* furniture delivery; breakfast meeting; car, train, bus, scooter broke down; funeral. Note to self: When faking funerals remember to wear black.

---

*Many princesses are superstitious about using the sick dog excuse after finding out that their dogs become sick one to twenty-four hours later.

3. Would pay in full the fees for therapy sessions / haircuts/gym classes that you've overslept through.
4. Have stopped planning sushi lunch dates because you can't handle raw fish as your first meal of the day.
5. Pay your assistant hush money to keep your morning tardiness quiet and to give you a wake-up call every morning until you're out of bed.
6. Have had your boyfriend wake you up after you've fallen back asleep on the toilet.
7. Carpool or take cabs to work so you can apply makeup on the way.

8. Use freight elevators and other service entrances so your boss and co-workers don't see you getting off the elevator at 10:45 A.M.
9. Make sure each night before you go home to leave your computer on with a coat and bag decoy at your desk to make co-workers think you've come in early the next morning.

are you an extreme pamperer?

Sports fans have the X-games. Princesses have extreme pampering. With the onslaught of so many beauty innovations, like chemical acid peels, non-bovine injectables, and Cool Glide lasers, experiencing beauty treatments (Is that smoke coming from my armpit!) can feel more daring than jumping from a heli-copter on a snowboard. Are you living life on the scalpel's edge? Take this quiz to find out.

1. Your definition of pampering is...

a. Me-time

b. Pain + adrenaline = no body hair

2. When you see a needle, you...

a. Faint

b. Write a check to your dermatologist for $500

3. You are addicted to...

a. Diet Coke

b. Lymphatic massage

79

continued

4. **Arrange the following treatments from least painful to most painful**

a. Cold waxing your pudendum

b. Electrolysizing the center of your upper lip

c. Waxing your calves

5. **You marked your passage into womanhood when you...**

a. Got your period

b. Bought your first jar of La Mer

6. **Which of the following would you describe as a sound investment...**

a. Real estate

b. Armpit electrolysis

7. **Your best friend is your...**

a. Dog

b. Magnifying mirror

Congratulations!
If you answered b and knew #4 was a trick question (they all hurt like hell),* then you are an Extreme Pampering Princess. You get your kicks by doing Botox shots—the beauty equivalent of bungee jumping—and think a triathlon is getting collagen, a Brazilian wax, and electrolysis in the same day.

One word of caution: Cher.

*Die-hard fans concur that the pain scale from least to most is: c, a, b.

Princess Challenge

Ask your therapist if you can bring
your manicurist to your next session
so you can kill two pampering birds with one stone.

FIVE

The Princess Pooch

*Every day I strive to be
the person my dog thinks I am.*

WINSTON CHURCHILL

MYTH:

All princesses treat dogs as fashion accessories.

REALITY:

Princesses are devoted to our dogs.
The reason we shower so much love and attention,
and so many outfits, on them is because they let us.

WHAT'S A telltale princess sign? A fresh manicure. But a dead giveaway? A manicured hand holding a leash. Princesses and dogs go together like parties and dresses, Belgium and chocolate, cabanas and terry cloth. It's not just because they make every outfit cuter (although they do). Princesses like dogs because they, above all other creatures, satisfy our need to pamper someone other than ourselves. Dogs lap up the constant doting, trendy outfits, belly rubs, and presents without giving us any attitude—ever. Other animals— cats, parrots, fish (or men and babies for that matter)— can be fussy, even downright cantankerous. Imagine taking a cat shopping on a leash, or dressing a man in a ladybug Halloween costume. It doesn't sound like fun, does it? However, dogs and princesses share a mutual relationship of indulgence: We become masters of shih tzu shiatsu and they give us an invaluable gift in return.

Until I got a dog I thought fame wasn't in the cards and E! was never coming to interview my friends in the sunrooms of their Malibu homes. But then my husband and I adopted a downy-white fluff-ball bichon frise we named Chewie (christened after the close personal friend of Princess Leia) and experienced instant fame by puppy proxy. I don't think I've ever seen the ASPCA run an ad that says: "Small dogs make you famous. Adopt one today." But it's true. Once, after he emerged from the groomer looking like a wagging cupcake, a burly, red-faced man, who could easily have accessorized his look with a lobster trap, got down on his hands and knees and greeted Chewie in baby talk. In Midtown, five fraternity-meets-Lehman-Brothers saw Chewie on the corner and sighed in unison as if they were twelve-year-olds at a petting zoo. Jogging past a playground, a pack of small children chased after us, causing their nannies to chase after them. During a late-night walk, a cabdriver slowed down and made kissing noises; I ignored the catcalls until he said "Nice dog" and drove off.

Chewie's breeder had urged us to show him. Both his parents had been champions, it would be a loss to the bichon breed, she said. But we didn't want a show dog, we wanted a pet and Chew needed a home. So we compromised: We own a show-off dog.

The Chewie frenzy got so overwhelming that I started to empathize with stars like Britney and Julia. Trying to deflect attention, I'd pop him in a bag. But this only made matters worse. A puppy is cute enough. A white, fluffy puppy in a bag is almost too much for people to bear. They'd see Chewie and be struck dumb. Strangers would lurch toward me like zombies, hands extended, saying "Furry!" I decided Mattel should market a bag with a cute dog's head sticking out so little girls could prepare for international celebrity.

Before we went out, I'd fluff Chew up, clean his eyes, and spritz him with lavender water. I wondered out loud if I was becoming one of those pageant mothers who feels good about herself by dressing her daughter up in miniature ball gowns and applying mascara to her four-year-old lashes. But I couldn't help myself, I was addicted to the attention. My friend Sadie noticed how much pleasure I took in all the fuss over Chew and wagged a cautionary finger: Your children will never be as cute as that dog. This is it for you.

I may not ever thank the Academy, or have to dodge the paparazzi at airports. But Chewie's been the canine equivalent of Henry Higgins. While I thought I was the one doing all the giving, he's taught me how to do the prom queen wave and handle compliments graciously. Would-be starlets heed my words: Your best publicist is a puppy.

PET DISCLAIMER

There are large, thriving populations of cat princesses, horse princesses, chinchilla-loving princesses, not to mention allergy-riddled princesses who can't have any pets (save for their grandmother's beaver stole). If you are one of these princesses, don't worry—you can still be a princess even if you don't have a puppy in your purse, and you can still get a lot out of this chapter. Simply substitute your boyfriend/cat/horse/chinchilla for all the dog references herewith.

QUIZ: *is your dog a princess, too?*

Choosing a dog isn't like picking out another cute accessory. A dog reveals more about you than your hair and purse combined. So not just any dog will do for a princess; you both have very specific love, grooming, and travel needs. Before you call the A.K.C., take the quiz below to discover which of the princess breeds is right for you.

1. Did you ever fantasize about becoming a hairdresser?

a. Yes
b. No
c. You are a hairdresser

2. Exercise for you is:

a. Long, solitary runs
b. Pumping up with personal trainer
c. Running in and out of cabs

3. Do you snack?

a. Yes
b. Does eating fat-free, lactose-free, sugar-free frozen yogurt count as a snack?
c. No

4. The last time you wore ruffles was...

a. Yesterday
b. 1983
c. The only ruffles I ever consider are in the potato chip aisle at the grocery.

5. You prefer water that's...

a. Sparkling
b. Iced with lemon
c. Fortified with electro-lytes

6. Your bag is...

a. Lighter than a pack of cigarettes
b. Bigger than a shoe box
c. Heavier than the September issue of *Vogue*

7. When you were a little girl you played with...

a. Dolls
b. Stuffed animals
c. Boys

SCORING

1. *a*, 1; *b*, 2; *c*, 3
2. *a*, 1; *b*, 2; *c*, 3
3. *a*, 3; *b*, 1; *c*, 2
4. *a*, 3; *b*, 1; *c*, 2
5. *a*, 3; *b*, 1; *c*, 2
6. *a*, 1; *b*, 2; *c*, 3
7. *a*, 3; *b*, 1; *c*, 2

(7 to 11 points) Fashion Hound

DOGS THAT LOOK GOOD IN SWEATERS

(Westies, Scotties, Yorkies, Jack Russells, Miniature Schnauzers, Corgis, Norwich and Norfolk Terriers)

You can't tell what's cuter, your dog or his hand-knit Fair Isle sweater. Though some fashion hounds can be too big to be carried in your handbag, they make up for it by having a build that is perfectly proportioned to wear slickers, fleece, and fishermen sweaters. Word of caution: Though you've never been a fan of couples who wear matching sweatshirts, you won't be able to resist buying matching Burberry trenches for you and your pup.

(12 to 17 points) Chic Chien

DOGS THAT LOOK GOOD IN COLLARS

*(Chihuahuas, Dachsunds,
Shar-Peis, Pugs, French Bulldogs,
King Charles Spaniels)*

These breeds can be the perfect couple compromise; their strong bodies appeal to men's desire for a tough-looking dog while their shiny, short coats cry out to be accessorized. Collars—jeweled especially—dazzle against sleek black or beige necks (they're also great candidates for turtlenecks). Added plus: Unlike fashion hounds that look best in preppy surroundings, and pretty poochies that require a few chandeliers (see next page), these neomodern breeds can be mixed and matched with Eames, chintz, or club chairs.

(18 and up) Pretty Poochie

DOGS THAT LOOK GOOD IN BAGS

(Bichons, Haveneses, Pomeranians, Papillons, Teacup Poodles, Shih Tzus, Malteses, Pekingeses, Silky Terriers, Toy Spaniels)

These breeds have descended from royal courts to warm laps, protect their owners from shopping alone, and faithfully carry on the love affair between pampered women and pampered dogs. Pretty poochies fit in just about any handbag, and some toy breeds are tiny enough to be carried in a pouch-shaped evening purse. Though their super-thick coats never need an extra layer, that doesn't stop princesses from swathing them in adorable sweaters and sable, even if it does make their fluffy heads look much too big for their bodies. Necessary daily grooming and a vast assortment of hair accessories will help bring out your inner hairdresser.

pet tips: choosing a name

If it's a girl: Call your dog Chanel and every bag will be a Chanel bag.

If it's a boy: Live the fantasy. Name him after your favorite leading man: Tom, Russell, Benecio. Or go for something more generic like "Boyfriend"—he'll never break up with you, and it's fun to give commands like "Bad Boyfriend" and "Boyfriend, sit."

 Warning: It might seem like more fun to name your dog after your real boyfriend ("Down, David") but this usually results in name-retraining every six months to a year and is not recommended.

The Characteristics of the Princess Dog

Slightly upturned nose
Was comforted as a pup by a ticking
clock wrapped in a cashmere sock sprayed
with your perfume. As a result,
he knows the difference
between Chanel #5 and
Chanel #19.

Satisfied expression
Princess dogs never need
to beg. They know that, with
that face, *all* will be given.

Taste
The princess breed's idea of dog
food is organic steak, chicken,
or lamb on a bed of jasmine rice
with a baby carrot salsa.

The charm collar
In lieu of V-chips, princesses use
jangling charms on collars to locate our
dogs at all times. Typical collar will have:
license, rabies status, and name tags (en-
graved with phone, address, sweater size),
various protective medallions, and a locket
with a lock of our hair and photo.

The collar
What handbags are to
princesses, comforters
are to college freshmen,
and engagement rings to
fiancées: that one small
strap barks volumes about
your dog's style, from
rhinestone to monogrammed
needlepoint.

Fur coat
Even if we object for ourselves, we think it looks great
on our dog.

Wagging tail
Princess dogs are happy.
Wouldn't you be if your life
had so much in common with
"I Dream of Jeannie"? Both
lounge around on silk pillows
all day, get whatever they want
just by blinking a certain way,
and run their masters' lives.

Jewelry and pedicures
Not just for bitches. No matter
what our boyfriends say, glittering
accessories and painted toes do not
emasculate already fluffy boy dogs.

Dog Training

MOTTO:

*"Everything your dog needs to know
he'll learn while shopping."*

Agility

- Rolls over to let customers and sales staff rub belly.
- Drinks out of paper cup in bathroom (on demand).
- Can jump over shopping bags (four deep).

Sportsmanship

- Sniffs, does not chew the merchandise.
- Does not mistake sensors for bones.
- Does not steal Peds from shoe salesmen.
- Usually behaves when sees other dogs, except during barking tantrums when security escorts you from the store.

Endurance

- Does not pee on clothes racks.

How a Princess Scoops Poop

Traveling in Style

Princess puppy mantra: "Don't leave home without him." Traditional dog carriers arouse suspicion; here's how we manage to sneak our dogs in everywhere.

The Bag: *Designer tote.*

Also known as the doyenne of doggy bags.
Caveat: Line bag with waterproof pad.

Best used for

a. **Airplanes:** placed under seat in front of you. CAUTION! Toy breed owners: Remember to take dog out of bag before putting bag through security X ray. P.S.: Build in time for security guards to fuss over puppy.

b. **Power lunches, casual dinners, dates (tie scarf, à la Grace Kelly, on handle, drape scarf over dog's head to get past maître d'):** Share your dinner with him. *Note:* Ordering a side of hamburger only creates suspicion.

c. **Office:** Smile your way past the security guards. Turn dog away from elevator camera. Make sure he doesn't pee in boss's office.

The Bag: *L.L. Bean Tote.*

A.k.a. The evergreen. This tote tricks everyone into thinking you're either an expert sailor or an academic. It's sturdy and comfortable whether your dog's head is tucked inside or peeking out over the top, and it can be color coordinated with outfits. Light cushion suggested (or swap for Pierre Deux quilted bag). L.L. Bean nineteen-inch models can be thrown over shoulder with winter coat on. Monogram required. *Caveat:* The bag is heavy, weighs approximately one and a half pounds. Thankfully, men don't mind carrying it.

Best used for

a. **Public transportation:** Get on buses, hail cabs, and glide on subways by strategically hiding dog's head.
b. **Supermarkets:** Place bag in cart, cover dog with bag of low-fat potato chips. When at deli counter, ask for a roast beef sample and slip him a taste.
c. **Therapy sessions:** Cheaper and less crazy than sending your dog to his own therapist.
d. **Houses of worship:** After all, dog spelled backward is God.
e. **Movies:** A must! French bulldogs and poodles are huge Truffaut fans.

The Bag: *Sac de paille.*

Translation: straw bag. First discovered while vacationing in Provence. Irresistible in bright fuchsia, puce, tangerine, and watermelon, especially those with cute gingham or polka-dot liners. *Caveat:* Though straw is lighter than leather and canvas, it's not safe for pudgy pups.

Best used for
Vacations and summer alternative to all of the above.

A WORD ABOUT WEIGHT

Princesses share an understanding: If our dog has a weight problem, we deny it, relying on the old adage "Puppy's not fat he's fluffy" (also applies to short-haired breeds). Hence, shoulder bruising, sciatica, and many other back problems go unchecked as we insist that nothing could be easier than carrying around our eighteen-pound dachshund.

Grooming

Chichi Fifi: The Natalie Woof of princess dogs, not only does she look pretty, she feels pretty. Fifi has her hair blown out more often than you do, is trained not to chew on recently clipped and painted nails, never goes out in the rain without her raincoat—and loves to travel Coach (the bag, that is).

Mr. Goodbark: Tries to run away from the dog salon every time you take him, and has been known to rub his freshly groomed body in horse excrement. He also enjoys being brushed nightly, basks in the warm wind when having hair blown out in the salon and at home, and submits to wearing ribbons, bandannas, or barrettes for up to six minutes after being groomed professionally—at least long enough for you to take a picture. Your only complaint: He suffers from raincoat intolerance (see next page).

Gnaw-T by Nature: The princess's worst nightmare. Gnaw-T chews hairbrushes to bits; rolls her body all over your couch after you spray her with lavender water; refuses to wear cute outfits, preferring to walk around naked. Sometimes you wonder how you ever ended up with a hippie for a dog. Her saving grace: She knows she can lick your face but not your eye cream.

raincoat intolerance

Many dogs suffer from Raincoat Intolerance, known as RI in princess circles. And though vets don't recognize RI and boyfriends encourage it, RI is a serious problem that threatens your dog's cuteness quotient.

RI is characterized by (a) complete paralysis when he wears raincoat, (b) chewing on coat, (c) laying down in coat and refusing to get up, and (d) backing away and hiding under bed or behind boyfriend as soon as raincoat is removed from closet.

Facing RI. First, ask yourself how important it is for your dog to wear a raincoat. If he's not a puppy, you may have lost your window of training opportunity and have to be content with just the cute sweaters, collars, charm collars, hair clips, fancy treats, dog beds, and bags available. Although there's no cure for RI, it can be prevented through raincoat conditioning in early life.

PHASE I:

Early Prevention: Put raincoat on puppy. Praise him. Reward him with treats and more praise. Initially have him wear coat indoors for only fifteen minutes. Introduce raincoat once a week and work your way up to once a day outside. (Pick days that look overcast so people don't stare.) Over time your puppy will learn to love his raincoat or get very fat trying.

PHASE II

Train your boyfriend to walk dog wearing raincoat.

Socialization

A page from the doggy datebook:

7:30 a.m.	Wake, stretch. Five minutes of puppy yoga, starting with downward dog
8:30 a.m.	Drop pup off at Bed and Biscuit Doggy Day Care.
	• We want our dog's social life to be as active as our own. So rather than leave him home all day, we enroll our dog in doggy day care—a canine country club that emphasizes good breeding, socializing, athleticism (some have gyms, pools, agility courses), and there's plenty of drinking.
3:30 p.m.	PetEx dog chauffeur picks up pup. Takes him to hair salon.
	• Excessive to some, necessary for us. Really it's less like a chauffeur and more like a puppy car pool.

5:50 p.m. Pick pup up from groomer.

- We see our dogs as extensions of ourselves. We know all their flaws and finer points and have combed, fluffed, and powdered them into perfection—or hired someone to do it. So when a friend makes an offhand comment like "Oh, he's got bad breath!" or "Has he put on a few?" it's personal.

5:55 p.m. Walk or drive home (puppy strapped in seat belt, head out the window, mindful not to tangle new hairdo) basking in the post-grooming glory.

- Princesses are cleared of all responsibility for people who trip, walk into poles, or have minor fender-benders while admiring her and her dog.

6:20 p.m Arrive home just before thunderstorm.

- *Maltese law:* If a princess dog has been groomed, it will rain within the next twenty-four hours.

Puppy Parties

The birthday party: Princesses don't make a big deal out of their dogs' birthdays. We just give them a bone and fill the toilet bowl with champagne.

The Halloween parade: We spend so much time designing our dog's Brad Pitbull costume that we barely have time to think up something for ourselves.

The holiday party: No matter how many gourmet treats and fluffy toys we fill their stockings with, we prepare for the fact that they really just want to eat the sock.

Fourth of July: This is the only holiday that we encourage our dogs to stay home and take a tranquilizer.

Princess Challenge

*Train your puppy to bring you your slippers
as well as your handbag.*

PART THREE

Your Reign

SIX

Princess Profashionalism

*You don't know it,
but I'm a vertical megabrand
with cross-media platforms.*

MYTH:

Princesses will work until we can find a rich man
who will take care of us.

REALITY:

Princesses work so that we can take care of ourselves.
We do, however, favor professional environments
that have great views, expense accounts,
and many parties.

THERE'S A THIN, Tiffany-blue line that separates princesses from our co-workers. While our colleagues consider themselves professional, we can describe our nine-to-five persona in a richer, slightly more spectacular way: We're profashional. Profashionalism is doing your job with a trademark style—from your persuasive plea bargaining tactics to your penchant for performing oral surgery in snakeskin stilettos. It's salaried savoir faire: a princess corporate merger of style and substance.

Like being freed from making copies, profashionalism is a skill that one learns with time. It's much more than being best-dressed, winning office popularity contests, keeping a jar of butterscotch candy on your desk, or drinking (and eventually sleeping) with one of the boys in accounting. It's a hard-skill set, like derivatives of banking. MIT engineers might express it in a mathematical equation as: experience + confidence × flair = profashionalism. On TV's "The West Wing," the character C.J. manages to project a calm veneer and sling pithy comebacks in the midst of a crisis in Haiti

113

while wearing pithy slingbacks. That's profashionalism. But profashionalism doesn't mean being constantly cool; it can also mean having a nervous breakdown with panache. (Count to three. Unleash wildly incisive monologue about your dysfunctional office. Take deep breath. Resume normal happy self.) Profashionalism is knowing how to cry at the office (walk to nearby park bench, shed tears, visit your local Sephora—or equivalent—to freshen up with free samples), how to wait on five hungry drunks and still get a tip (tell bartender to water down drinks, faux-flirt with chef to rush entrees), or how to handle a $47 million flop at the box office (the same way you handle a success: Call each member of your team and thank them for their hard work).

At its best, profashionalism is imperceptible and omnipresent: If you're a funny gal, you tend to win over clients with your witty sense of humor. At its worst, you look like you're trying too hard to be unique: You insist on doing all your correspondence with a hot-pink pen. Some popular types of profashionals are:

Ms. Who-knew: Typically, this princess's immense skill and experience can be camouflaged by her being pretty, shy, short (under five-two), soft-spoken, young or old—yet she's consistently named the employee-of-the-month, much to the surprise of her more high-profile co-workers. *Example:* Hello Kitty.

Ms. Perfect: This princess overcompensates for some real or perceived flaw by making sure that whatever she does—law, brain surgery, cat grooming—is done flawlessly. Her work can be described in one word: Butter. *Example:* Barbra Streisand.

Ms. Reinvention: This charismatic chameleon princess sheds her iconic image every few years to transform into a new version of herself. She cycles through roles—vixen to activist, mother to yoga guru—in a matter of months. But the key to success is that with each new incarnation she still continues to be appealing—and profitable— filling her office/recording studios/campaign headquarters with her talented entourage and large bouquets of flowers from presidents, fans, lobbyists. *Examples:* Madonna, Hillary Clinton.

Profashionalism at Work

Regardless of your interpretation, all profashionals share the following qualities.

A keen sense of awareness: Profashionals know that CEO is in the details—and naturally, notice everything, from the stacks of unopened mail on the boss's desk (a clue she has a disorganized assistant) to eye-rolling in meetings (internal disputes). On a micro level we'll track when high-level executives log on and off instant messenger (we cleverly decipher user names). And on a macro level we can use our powers of observation in the market, like the financial analyst profashional who predicted the demise of a biotech company after she attended a meeting on-site and noticed that they used expensive Charmin toilet tissue companywide. Fellow analysts denounced her as an alarmist. But she knew that with marginal profits and high overhead they were doomed. Four months later they announced they were filing for Chapter Eleven.

An appreciation of presentation: Depending on where we work, profashionals are known to decorate our offices with special accents like flowering plants or Tibetan daybeds. We make great first impressions; our résumés are printed on colored and/or scented paper. Thank-you notes are clever and well crafted. On the job, we can reduce a nine-hundred-page monograph to a sixty-page outline, then thirty, then fifteen, then cards—and they are color-coordinated. We rehearse pitches in teams at the office and again at home in front of our pets. We obsess over our projects, causing colleagues to call us all sorts of names—Power-point perfectionists and the Colin Cowie of accounting—to our face. Our motto: Don't hate us because our work is beautiful.

A knack for networking: In a testament to our social skills, our Rolodexes and birthday parties get bigger every year. We find other profashionals the same way we find everything—through a friend. Our high friendship retention rate makes us privy to all sorts of insider information. In recent deal-making news: A profashional account executive at a world-renowned ad agency was having breakfast with a headhunter princess who mentioned that a competitive company was planning to acquire a small, hip agency to help lure sexier accounts. It just so happens that the small, hip agency was where the account executive got her start and the president was a friend from her yogalaties class. By lunchtime she'd pitched the acquisition idea to her boss and a month later was closing the deal for her company to acquire the hot-shop over wheat grass shots at the gym juice bar. Profashional moral of the story: Making money with friends is even more fun than spending money with friends.

A dash of resilience: Profashionalism is easy in good times, but what about in bad? Consider the fable of a fired CEO: A woman who had been touted as a leader of the feminization of the workplace was sacked two rocky years after taking over as the head of a high-profile corporation. When the ax came down, phones rang. Rumors flew. The industry snickered. Her shocked close-knit staff stood around in clumps—some crying as they watched her collect her things. Two weeks later, she invited the entire staff to a dinner party at her house. It was lavish with free-flowing champagne, figs, and large chunks of Parmesan for starters. Everyone came together like a family—drank, ate, danced. She gave herself and her staff what she could not offer on that awful Friday afternoon with a security guard waiting at her door: closure. As each of her staff said good-bye, one manager said to another, "If I ever blow it, I'm throwing a party."

Profashionalism is what will make clients, colleagues, and friends ask to work with you. It's not just because you always look great, it's because you approach your job with an effortlessness that can only come from strategic planning, rigorous research, and a knack for knowing where to get a great martini even in the wee hours. Remember, for a profashional, it's not how glamorous your job is, it's how glamorously you do it.

The Profashional's Glossary

Administrative tasks: The secret to surviving as an assistant is understanding that menial tasks have hidden benefits. Expense reports double as your personal *Zagat* guide. Opening mail equals free stuff. Don't fret, your grunt work earns you points (think of it like frequent flier mileage: Eventually, it'll add up to your ticket out of there).

Advancement: Princesses take career and salary risks; we move from book publishing to television, television to education, full-time to freelance, corporate to nonprofit. And why not? Grace Kelly went from simply acting like a princess to being one.

Attitude: Don't pout when your great ideas are stolen by higher-ups. Think of yourself as the professional equivalent of collagen injections for your boss: You exist to make her look good, but everyone knows her secret.

Bathroom: Eventually you will have to go. It takes at least six months for a princess to pee comfortably in the bathroom with another employee. Some princesses have been known to use bathrooms on entirely separate floors from their workstations. You bring your own atomizer air fresheners into the stall. You wash your hands, but never touch the soap or soap dispenser—it's too dirty. You get paper towels by using your elbow to pull down the tab, keeping freshly washed hands uncontaminated. Fix face. Place paper towel over bathroom door handle. Exit.

Beaujolais Nouveau: Give a bottle of the fruity, inexpensive table wine to the folks in office services during the holidays and you'll never have a mail, phone, or computer problem—even when Mercury is in retrograde.

Crazy bosses: You will end up working for insane people—at least once. You may not like it, but as a profashional you recognize its advantages. *One:* You'll learn how underhanded, manipulative politics work without necessarily employing them yourself. *Two:* You'll feel superior for being sane in comparison. *Three:* You'll make some of your best friends (you become closer to your colleagues with each of their psychotic breakdowns). And *four:* You'll get loads of horrifying yet hilarious stories to entertain friends with at happy hour.

Crying: Make it work for you. Really, there's no room for tears at the office, but if you're a crier you should master: the silent cry in the bathroom—pick a favorite stall and sniffle it out; the parking lot bawl—hold back tears until you can get in your car; and the untraceable cube weep—pretend to be on the phone or looking for something under your desk and sob quietly so no one will disturb you. If accidentally caught crying, some princesses will kill off an already dead relative to throw nosy/concerned co-workers off the cry-baby trail.

Downsized: Getting fired is the universe's way of saying that a particular job was the professional equivalent of a bad perm. Your mother, your boyfriend, your best friend could have told you that it wasn't you, but you had to see for yourself.

Evil: Trust your instincts. Buffy the Vampire Slayer gets cramps in the presence of blood-sucking vampires; profashionals become involuntarily bulimic around backstabbers, too.

Freak-outs: Throwing tantrums on a regular basis makes them meaningless. If you must do your diva act, use it sparingly, like body glitter, for more impact.

Friendship: Don't worry too much about whether your co-workers like you. If you can do your job well, they'll respect you—and that's enough. Having friends at work is nice, but it's not the reason you're there. Think of office socializing as a surprising extra, like a free gift from Clinique.

Humility: As you move up, face the fact that your assistant makes fun of you the way you made fun of your boss, even though you're much cooler than your old boss and gave her the name of your psychic.

Image paradox: Just because you finally got the job you've been dreaming about—the offices are cool, your co-workers dress really well, and you love to tell people what you do for a living—doesn't guarantee you'll like working there.

Interviewing: Being prepared means you spend as much time researching the company as shopping for an outfit to wear. P.S.: No matter how "super-friendly" the interviewer is, complaining about your current job by saying things like "Oh my God, every day is worse than an aerobics class in hell" will not get you hired.

Managing: No matter how mature your staff is, they'll think of you as a mother figure. And depending on how they feel about their moms, you can be cast as Auntie Mame or Mommie Dearest. There's nothing you can do but be your fab self.

Quitting: Never quit in a huff. The most satisfying resignation is casually announcing you are moving on to a more meaningful, fulfilling, and satisfying job ("I'm leaving to rule a small Mediterranean country").

Success: After a job well done, profashionals will celebrate with an exotic vacation where they can congratulate themselves with piña coladas and ponder a deep profashional question: "So now what?"

Zero: What you will get if you don't ask for a raise, promotion, bigger office, four-day week, expense account, vacation, grant, think tank, and whatever else it takes to pursue your dream.

Relaxing rosemary-scented candle —unlit ever since that nasty accident with the help desk guy's braid when he was fixing your laptop

Lamps from home No one, not even a princess, looks good in fluorescent lighting

Black cashmere cardigan We're not ice princesses, just freezing-cold princesses

Antique chair with velvet or exotic seat cushion

Slippers for relief from stilettos

Cute personal stationery for sending congratulatory notes when a colleague at another company enjoys some success (you don't think of the competition as the enemy, but as your next employer)

1. You've had tickets to the ballet for months. On the night of the performance your office is in the midst of a project and it looks like it's going to be an all-nighter. You...

a. Ask your supervisor to make an exception for you, assuming your team will just have to understand.

b. Cancel plans and bitch about it all night.

c. Call client services and see if they have any clients who would appreciate your seventh-row-center seats. Then ensure they return the favor next week.

d. Instantly develop a stomach virus and excuse yourself.

2. You're trapped in a meeting and can't meet your boyfriend at the restaurant. You...

a. Excuse yourself to go to the bathroom and disappear for an hour and a half.

b. Make boyfriend wait alone at restaurant bar; your career comes first.

c. Ask assistant to call boyfriend and tell him you're stuck in a meeting but could he please meet you at your place in two hours, then surprise him by ordering his favorite dishes from the restaurant and have them delivered.

d. Get a sudden migraine and excuse yourself.

3 It's 7:30 and your team is about to order dinner. You...

a. Announce that you want something healthy, good, and quick but that you have no money so someone else has to pay.

b. Don't order and complain when the food arrives that they'll never get the smell of curry out of the conference room.

c. Charge dinner for team on corporate account, plus an extra dessert for housekeeping (because you asked her to wait to vacuum your hall until you left).

d. Diagnose yourself with typhoid and excuse yourself.

4 In a meeting where you are discussing the tactical strategy behind a new marketing plan that you've rewritten three times (the director's way, your way, and a bad combination of the two), the director asks why you didn't follow her suggestions. You...

a. Sit there dumbfounded and say you thought you did.

b. Defensively point to your boss and say she made you change it!

c. Take a breath, and then ask both of them if the three of you could put your tiaras together to come up with a marketing plan that works for everyone.

d. Flare up with prickly heat and excuse yourself.

125

continued

5. The upside to working late is...

a. The satisfaction of meeting the deadline and making your client happy.
b. Earning overtime.
c. Knowing there are three ways to bond at the office—working late, drinking, and gossiping—which is why you like to mix late nights with nightcaps to get the best dish.
d. Perfecting your acting craft of coming down with sudden illnesses.

Scoring

The correct answer to all of the above is c. Of course, being princesses, we judiciously use d. Proof that when the going gets tough, the tough know how to make themselves an exception.

Is She or Isn't She?

How to tell if the new girl is a profashional:

1. Her color-coordinated boxes arrive two days before she does.

2. She hugs half the office when her boss gives her the tour. Typically, new profashionals already know their co-workers from previous jobs, the gym, and book club.

3. She receives so many bouquets her office looks like a wake—most common in fashion and beauty industry. *Note:* Some junior-level profashionals have been known to send themselves flowers and say they are from previous employers.

4. Two brawny men arrive to move furniture and install deluxe air purifier. The walls are painted and carpet cleaned for the first time in fifteen years. How does she get this to happen? Every profashional knows that a new boss will indulge a new employee for the first three days of her career. The profashional move-in mantra: "Speak now or forever sit with your desk facing the wall."

5. She's dressed well but not overdressed. First days on the job (and when breaking up with someone) call for low-key looks. A profashional likes her fashion to peak midweek, when people begin to notice her.

Princess Challenge

*Apply for the buyer position at Neiman Marcus and list
"Can pick out cute gifts for God" under special skills.*

SEVEN

Princess Entertains

Life is what happens
while you're making party plans.

MYTH:
Princesses throw parties
to be the center of attention.

REALITY:
Princesses are always
the center of attention—
even when we're home alone.

WHEN IT COMES to princess parties, our birthday is, of course, our favorite. But for the 364 days of the year that are not dedicated exclusively to celebrating our own existence, princesses know the purpose of entertaining is not just to surround yourself with good friends and good food, it's having a secret agenda.

GETTING SCOOP

The most popular agenda is reconnaissance, or what we call "an information gathering." It's the princess version of the Magic 8-Ball. We want answers. We throw a party to shake things up and see what happens. For one summer my friend Ann and I were actually double-agent hostesses. We assigned ourselves the mission after Ann got tired of going on second dates with guys who turned out to be living at home, closet alcoholics, or ex-managers of Kiss. We decided that *before* she agreed to the second and usually lengthier dinner date, we'd

throw an information gathering* so we could do some potential-relationship research. I invited friends, she invited friends, and we'd observe the second-date candidate in a natural bar setting. We never revealed our double-agent-hostess status to anyone (until now), and we saved Ann from a number of unnecessary bikini waxings.

---

*The "Is he worth a second date?" agenda is just one of hundreds of information gatherings. They can be used to find out anything—great real estate deals about to go on the market, fluctuations in the pork belly futures, who's having an affair with whom in the neighborhood—but personal love agendas are the most popular. Another romantic reconnaissance agenda is the "Is he interested?" party. A princess will decide to have a party so she can invite her current crush. If he attends, she's halfway there. (Married friends are keen to host these parties for their single friends.) Still, every "Is he interested?" party should have a backup agenda, like "How cute is Alyssa's brother?" in case Bachelor #1 is a no-show. And every princess knows that his arrival is not a guarantee. Depending on his clothes and his response to your crudités, the soiree could shift from "Is he interested?" into an "Is he gay?" party.

Dressing Up

Nothing is lonelier than a cocktail dress without an occasion, which leads us to another princess party agenda:
dressing up. Chiffon dresses, sexy jeans, and bejeweled
sandals all look better when they're accessorized with an
invitation. We could be browsing in a no-buy zone, but
as soon as we see something cute we end up performing
the princess party trick: justifying any purchase by
thinking up an instant occasion. (It doesn't matter that
we already have three outfits for said occasion.) Creative
types will declare next Tuesday "Tiara Tuesday!" and
host cocktails. It's also no coincidence that some
princesses throw parties around the same time a new
shipment of Marc Jacobs hits the stores.

CELEBRATING AN ACCOMPLISHMENT

Personal milestones are always good reasons for princesses to plan a luau. Self-congratulatory parties run the gamut from celebrating our return from a spa or breaking up with our boyfriend to a conversion to Sufism. Princesses use discretion when revealing the motive for the self-congratulatory party. If we've just run the New York City Marathon, we'll definitely say so. This way guests will know why we're receiving them on a chaise longue. If we're celebrating our final lip and chin electrolysis appointment, we'll just wear sexy red lipstick and forget to dim the lights.

GUILT-FREE REDECORATING

The eternal princess question: Which came first, the urge to redecorate or the cute invitations? It doesn't matter if we start small with plastic dishes and a few votive candles; our planning can quickly escalate to include purchasing a chandelier and repainting the house (interior and exterior). Princesses understand that home furnishings, like the bones of the human skeleton, are all connected: Touch one and it sends shock waves throughout the entire body of an apartment. New rugs are connected to new pillows and new pillows lead to new slipcovers, and on and on. Spy a princess in Pottery Barn and you can be guaranteed a party will be delivered in four to six weeks between the hours of eight and eleven.

Forget goodie bags, the princess party favor of choice is sex. What's nice about the sex agenda is that it can be attached to any party and extends to both hostesses and guests (see box).

Hostesses (married, dating, or single) all have the same sexual agenda. The real question is when. Married princesses prefer to have it before the party, in lieu of a glass of merlot, a nap, or nibbling on pigs in a blanket, which explains their party glow. Single hostesses usually have their party favor after the party with the sweet boy who tells his friends he'll "stay and help clean up."

GUEST SEX AGENDAS

Princess guests have different sexual agendas than princess hostesses. Single princess guests aren't looking to have sex that evening (weddings are the exception), but rather the promise of sex. The contents of their goodie bag are flirtatious banter, kisses in the hallway with a cute guy, and a date for next Friday.

Princess guests with dates, meanwhile, get goo-goo eyes across the room from their date, a passionate cab ride home, and a diary entry of late-night fun.

Married princess guests can look forward to un peu de tout—the flirting (with husband and other men at party, evidence that you've still got it), a guarantee date who takes you home to bed, plus the matchmaker's bonus: the promise that two people you introduce will hook up that night.

137

And last but not least, the opportunity to open presents in the eleven nonbirthday months is always extra incentive for a princess to break out the cheese logs. We know that there are no small presents, just small boxes. So whatever the occasion—engagement, puppy showers, housewarming (some princesses will move just to redecorate and get presents)—there are three words that will never appear on a princess's party invitation: *No gifts, please.*

are you a princess hostess?

1. You prefer the role of...

a. Crasher
b. Guest
c. Hostess
d. All of the above

2. You're most likely to host...

a. Tuesday-night cocktails
b. Friday-night buffet
c. Saturday-evening gala
d. All of the above

3. Your party wouldn't be complete without...

a. Cheese bought in bulk
b. A catfight
c. An ice sculpture
d. None of the above

4. You hire a cleaning woman the day...

a. After the party
b. Of the party
c. Before the party
d. All of the above

5. Your lover helps you with the party by...

a. Zipping you up
b. Setting up the bar
c. Bringing at least one eligible bachelor
d. All of the above

SCORING

Mostly A's, Well-meaning Beginner: Tired of the sorority mixer? Good. Because unless your friends are freshmen, they're outgrowing your parties. Your college-party deprogramming includes reading the classics *Tiffany's Table Manners for Teenagers* and *Emily Post's Entertaining* (we must know the rules in order to break them). Then go to Blockbuster to return your *Animal House* DVD and rent the following films: *The Party, La Dolce Vita,* and *Who's Afraid of Virginia Woolf.* Until you complete your studies, stick to throwing "after-parties." This way your guests will be too tipsy to notice that after sitting on your couch their bums are completely covered in cat hair.

Mostly B's, Anxious Intermediate: Overwhelmed with the burden of being responsible for everyone's good time you (a) drink too much and fall down, (b) have a fight with your boyfriend, (c) forfeit your role as hostess and let guests fend for themselves. What's the matter? Your mother's not invited so stop acting like someone is going to criticize you. The truth is you've done everything right: You ordered mini-champagne bottles and straws, watched Nigella all week, and called the caterer. The only thing you forgot to do was to take a pill (metaphorically or literally). A good hostess knows that anyone can pretend to have made the shrimp puffs, but only a pro can pretend to be relaxed.

Mostly C's, Casually Advanced: If life's a party then you're the girl to throw it. The key to your party success is that you throw them about every six weeks. Practice equals a perception of effortlessness. You have a system: You keep a record of what you served at each event. You have your local liquor store on speed dial. And stock up on extra piñatas if things get dull. The trick is prepping the details weeks in advance. Why, just yesterday morning you were up at six A.M. rolling goat cheese balls in minced herbs, Windexing the chandelier, trimming your hedges into circus topiaries, dusting the drapes, and vacuuming the walls (or telling your manservant to do it). But you'd give up your preparty massage before you'd cop to it. The golden rule of hostessing: Never reveal how much you did for the occasion. Every good party has some mystery. Your soirees leave guests wondering: *Does she or doesn't she have hired help?*

Mostly D's, Seasoned Professional: You've actually stopped throwing your own parties. You outsource your elaborate to-do lists and arrive as a hostess figurehead.

How a Princess Knows She's Thrown a Good Party

- All the people from your last party come plus one.

- You were able to sit still for at least five minutes and talk to your boyfriend, meaning everyone had been introduced, had a full glass, and was chatting with someone new.

- Your matchmaking schemes actually worked.

- You have celebrity crashers: Someone brings along Luke and Owen Wilson.

- There's a huge pile of stilettos next to the dance floor.

- The police come and leave with a few hors d'oeuvres.

- There's not a drop of bubbly or a crumb of crudité left.

- Guests gush all over you when they finally do leave.

- People stay so late you change from your sexy party dress to your silk party pajamas—and they still don't go home.

- You go to bed with a new laugh line from smiling so much.

- The next day friends call for a postmortem on who was smooching whom; what was up with that girl in the pleated and cropped pants; who's cuter, Luke or Owen Wilson; and when are you doing it again?

- You get clever thank-you notes. For example: "Dear Princess, Thanks for the fabulous party! If you find a pair of polka-dot boxers they're mine!"

- You hear about your party from someone who wasn't there.

- Your mailbox is flooded with invitations to upcoming galas.

Princess Challenge

*Use your next party as an excuse to execute the
stay-at-home move.*

Step 1: Pick a date for the party.
Step 2: Make a list of all the things you'd like to rearrange.
*Step 3: Spend the next two weeks purging and
redecorating until your first guests ring the doorbell.*

EIGHT

Prince Charming

Men are dogs you
can't put in your purse.

MYTH:

Princesses expect men to
provide our happily-ever-after.

REALITY:

Princesses do not look to men
to turn our lives into fairy tales;
we've figured out how to
do it for ourselves.

PRINCESSES APPROACH dating as if we're clothes shopping. We've updated "there's a lid for every pot" with "there's a sarong for every bikini." It's not such a stretch. Haven't you noticed the similarities between personal ads and catalog copy? "Body hugging, great for a workout or snuggling up on the couch. Available in black, white, or tan." Now, of course, princesses don't *really* go around classifying men as clothing purchases. But it does make the idea of dating seem a lot more fun, like something you'd actually want to do on a rainy Friday night. We want to know what our dates are made of: Is he a 100 percent genuine gentleman or a blend of 25 percent player and 75 percent hair gel? Is that older man *vintage* or just *used*? Over the course of our lives, princesses mentally try on hundreds of guys, but take only a few home. Even after we're married we still shop for "presents" for our friends.

Savvy shoppers that we are, we've classified men into four distinct categories: impulse purchases, luxury items, flattering basics, and one-of-a-kinds.

Category

The Impulse Buy

Your exposure to the impulse buy depends on your promiscuity. If you're a serial monogamist, it's likely that less than 3 percent of your romances fall into this category. However, if you attend a single-sex college and only meet guys at frat parties, your exposure can be a whopping 90 percent. The impulse buy is also known as dating for amusement. These are the men you tell funny stories about at parties. You know right away that this boy is not going to be your everyday bag. He's more like a $5 glittering clutch from H&M that you bought for New Year's Eve.

How to recognize him: You give him a nickname. Very rarely do you remember his real name; instead, you christen him with a pet name based on some memorable fact: the cowboy guy, the ugly guy, lefty, or, simply, the twenty-four-year-old.

He's a novelty: He's a train conductor, a redhead, a German painter, a bartender.

You make an exception: Things that would normally be deal breakers only add to your attraction: He's only in town

152

for a few days. He doesn't speak English. He has a girl-friend. He was graduating junior high when you were graduating college. Your parents would hate him.

It's unexpected: You had no intention of hooking up, and you're wearing the underpants to prove it. You haven't shaved your legs for days. Your bed is covered in dirty laundry. You have to leave for a business trip at five o'clock the next morning.

Princess testimonial: "I met Charlie at a dimly lit bar. He was cute, curly-haired, and made excellent selections on the jukebox. He introduced himself as a stockbroker who had a house in the Hamptons. Three drinks later, he admitted that he was only twenty-three and had just landed his first job trading on the floor, and his parents had a house in the suburbs with an aboveground pool. I told him that his baby face gave him away, and that I didn't like the Hamptons anyway. I changed the subject by telling him I just got Nintendo. He suggested we go back to my place and play. Despite the seven-year difference I couldn't resist. Charlie was like a cute baby-T near the checkout counter. There was no need to try him on—I was happy to take him home and return him the next day if necessary. Which I did."

—*Sarah, New Jersey*

The catch: Know his limits. All that great sex is not going to turn your baby-T into a wedding dress.

Category 2

THE LUXURY ITEM

He's not just a wealthy investment banker, he's a gentleman whose cachet is more attractive than his cash.

How to recognize him: **He's a status symbol. He's a member of the Olympic crew team, the author of a crossover best-seller, a politician, a cutting-edge architect, a real estate mogul, a methadone-addicted rock star.**

He's hard to locate: **You have to go through his assistant, his manager, the hotel concierge, and three time zones to leave a message on his satellite phone.**

He's well known: **He impresses people who don't even know you, inspires envy in your best friend, and has a wait list (for clients and lovers).**

He's a one-name man: **As with the store-bought variety, you refer to your luxury item only by his first name—for instance, "Ralph is on his way over." Last names are used only when you're angry. "I can't believe Valentino said that!" And in some cases just his initials will do: "I think that's C.K. at the bar..."**

He's got great packaging: In the same way that many people shop at Tiffany & Co. for their signature turquoise shopping bag, the luxury item comes wrapped with backstage passes, custom-made suits, a view from the penthouse, literary roundtables, six-pack abs.

Princess testimonial: "I overheard this guy at a cocktail party telling someone about a party he had thrown for a well-known celebrity at his beach house in Malibu. Those three words—Malibu beach house—made me laugh to myself. Who are you? A Ken doll? As it turned out, yes, except his name was Tim. He was an up-and-coming movie producer with light brown hair and a laser-bright smile. He offered to walk me home on a chilly night and protectively tucked me under his arm to make sure I was on the inside of the street. We dated all winter while he worked on a picture. Tim was like a sable coat with my initials embroidered inside. I never thought I'd have one, and then here he was with his arms around me. He was warm. Irresistible. Other girls stared. I was sure I was falling in love. But as the filming wore on I felt suffocated by his schedule (four A.M. wake-up calls) and his scene (publicists strongly recommending that he eat with certain people in certain restaurants, and then Tim strongly recommending that I not be seen eating at all). When spring arrived the picture wrapped and I knew it was time to move on and put him in storage."

—*Louisa, New York City*

The catch: Your luxury item may not last more than a season or two.

Category ③

THE FLATTERING BASIC

What you don't realize is that the average flattering basic has the potential to be the black turtleneck Sharon Stone wore to the Academy Awards. But it's your job to recognize his untapped potential.

How to recognize him: You don't know him, but you feel as if you've met him before. You realize it's because he talks, walks, and dresses like all the guys on the commuter train, in your office cafeteria, and at the gym.

He's flexible: You can take him anywhere. He can easily transition from a baseball game to a cocktail party. He can mingle with the girls from your feminist studies book club and the gang from your oncology seminar.

He's quality merchandise: He's comfortable. Well built. Reliable. Uncomplicated. And you look great together.

Princess testimonial: "I never thought of Harry, my downstairs neighbor, in any romantic way. You know, he was just a guy, like a Harry Pothead type. But when the electricity went out one night, during a thunderstorm, we ended up talking for hours by candlelight. I realized he was a real find, like a perfect pair of jeans: comfortable but sexy, down-to-earth but cool. I had thought he was just an ordinary guy, but it turned out that he had been a professional surfer and now had a booming surfboard business. He goes back to Hawaii every spring to teach surfing privately at his parents' retreat in Hana. I couldn't stop trying on his life—coconut and mango smoothies for breakfast, then a day catching some waves. It's only the beginning, but I'm sure I'll love him even when he's old and tattered."

—*Elizabeth, San Francisco*

👑 *The catch:* With so many cheap imitations it's easy to take the real thing for granted. Don't. Your flattering basic is tough, but deserves TLC. Even jeans can go to the dry cleaner.

Category 4

ONE-OF-A-KIND

One percent! Yes, he's rare. But when he's the right one, he's all you need.

How to recognize him: You notice him right away. Just as your eagle eye can spot the last pair of size-ten Gucci pumps at a sample sale, you can walk into a bar, a library, the supermarket and just sense that you're in the presence of your soul mate.

He evokes an emotional response: Usually nausea—just looking at him makes your stomach do back flips.

You move fast: **Princesses know when to think things through—and this is not one of those times. You charged that handmade silk lingerie set in that little shop in Paris without asking the price, now you blindly take the seat next to him at the bar.**

Princess testimonial: **"When I first met my husband— a punk rocker with all the sweetness of a Hummel figurine—I was filled with the same giddy excitement as discovering a mint-condition Hermès Birkin bag at a flea market. He was in a class by himself, an authentic luxury item with the modesty of a flattering basic and the sex appeal of an impulse buy. I snatched him up."**
—The author, New York City

The catch: **You know he really is a one-of-a-kind when he feels the same way about you.**

Princess Dating 101

DRESSING

You: Not too sexy and not too sweet—you know you're ready to go out when you can look in the mirror and say to yourself, yeah, I'd want to have sex with me.

Him: A man should not be prettier than a princess. He should look casually undone. Too many designer labels are far worse than having none at all. Theme sweaters, acid-wash jeans, and decorative zippers equal death. And if he wears gold chains, fuggedaboudit.

EATING

You: Common sense tells you that if a woman doesn't feel comfortable eating in front of a man, she's not going to feel comfortable having an orgasm in front of him either. You order appetizers and dessert.

Him: Dining turnoff: Refusing to wait to be seated and going to a half-dozen restaurants until you find a dump with an empty table. Spontaneity is good, but reservations are better. **P.S.:** Adding salt to everything before he tastes it is a sign he's not so good in bed.

You: You don't want to hear about the past love of his life. By the same token, you refrain from gushing about your pet at length.

Him: If he says things like, "Did I tell you about me and that time that me, myself, and I were out at this bar," you know he's already in love with himself. But if he's not entirely self-involved you expect him to talk about:

1. His work. He should be able to make it sound interesting even if it's not.
2. How nice you look—and being you that should be easy.
3. His hobbies. Cooking? Good. You imagine coming home to delicious meals that he never expects you to clean up. Painting? Good. You imagine yourself as his muse. Dungeon master? Not good. You imagine weekends at sci-fi conventions.
4. His friends. You listen closely to those "crazy kegger" stories to see if his pals are: date-rapists, drug-addled, immoral embezzlers, or cuter than him.

PAYING

Guys pay. It's not about chivalry; it's about fiscal equality. See following list.

· Projected Princess Dating Costs

Mani: $10

Pedi: $20

Bikini wax: $17 *(if Brazilian add $50)*

Lip, brow, chin: $40

Bra and panties: $75

Birth control: $30 a month

Blow-out: $30

New dress: $150

Perfume: $1.60 (a few spritzes from one $100 bottle)

Dry cleaning: $20

Grand total $445.60. Even when you deduct 25 percent as the cost of self-maintenance and another 25 percent for other dates you may have that week, you are still contributing $222.80 to the evening—significantly more than the cost of an upscale dinner in most cities, plus a man's haircut. Fair is fair. Guys pay.*

---

*Princesses should buy a round of drinks at the bar, and many have been known to be generous contributors to the adorable musician, painter, law student boyfriend fund.

The one moment where princess and Disney are on the same page: There must be magic in that kiss. If not, you walk home humming Shania Twain's "I Shaved My Legs for This?"

Princess Crushes

Princesses have more crushes than there are shades of red lipstick. A sampling of our collections:

The conversational crush: You make great debate together. Other people call this friendship. And they're right. But there's just something about his banter that feels like verbal foreplay.

The clothing crush: You don't know him, but you want his sweater.

The canine crush: Your dog has a crush on a dog with a cute owner.

The e-mail/Instant Message crush: Double entendres lead to double dates. The e-mail crush is the equivalent of a conversational crush for literary types.

The title crush: You don't want his body, you want his job.

The apartment crush: It's much easier for you to fall in love with his prewar three-bedroom, two-and-a-half-bath with original moldings than with him.

The summer-house crush: Princesses don't sleep their way to the top...just to the beach.

Postbridal crush: The wedding pictures have been developed, you've unwrapped that last gift, and you feel as if you have nothing to look forward to. Enter the UPS man...

The bored-at-work crush: You find renewed passion for your job by developing a crush on a co-worker, prompting you to dress up for work more and feel generally cuter.

The Dating Coach

Diamonds, expensive underwear, and adorable boys can all scramble the princess mind. Luckily for us, there are paste, sales, and dating coaches. A dating coach is a friend in a serious relationship, preferably married, who can see past your crush's blue eyes, doctorate, and flirtatious e-mails to provide honest, tactful, and agenda-free dating advice. This person is not your mother. Ask your dearest, most trusted, and currently-in-a-relationship girlfriend to raise her right hand and repeat after you.

• THE DATING COACH PLEDGE •

I, the Dating Coach (insert name here)...

1. *Will escort you to parties or functions where there may be cute boys. This includes stuffy uptown bars, dingy Irish pubs, and crunchy environmental discussions even when I'm wearing fur.*

2. Will tell you when you have too much cleavage or not enough. Will road-test water bra on boyfriend/husband before letting you try yours on a new date.

3. Will strike up a conversation with your crush at a party, mentioning my boyfriend/husband in first five minutes then casually bring up an area of your expertise and hand him over to you, but remain in the conversation for two minutes to assess his eye contact and flirting.

4. Casually observe his "player" quotient by comparing how he talks to you and other women at the party and give you a play-by-play of his every move, down to how long he spent in the bathroom and who makes his shirts.

5. Will subtly inquire about your crush's romantic status while giving him vague but intriguing insight into yours.

6. Will engage in a post-party recap the following morning to review the highlights of the evening, such as "Yes, he kept glancing over at you." "No, the girl in the Lilly Pulitzer pants was his sister." "Yes, I think he's adorable, and that story about the monkey stealing his shorts in Bali was hilarious."

7. Will help you decipher what he really means when he leaves the message "Last night was nice."

8. Will refuse to let you sit by the phone by distracting you with mani/pedi appointments. Will line up dates with other men for you so that you're not planning your wedding by the third date.

9. Will be as obsessed with your romantic life as you are. No time is inconvenient, no detail too small to indulge in rela-

tionship analysis. Will leave cell phone on for date post-mortem, where I will interject "Sooo cute" after each activity. (Or "Eww" if he turns out to be Mr. Wrong.)

10. Will drop whatever I'm doing at work to listen as you read his e-mails over the phone and agree that his messages are: loaded with innuendo, entertaining, or prophetic. Will brainstorm clever banter to write back.

11. Will let you bash him when you break up (not the other way around) and provide at least one adorable college friend to help you get over him.

12. Will refuse to let you believe that you'll end up like one of those old society matrons who has to hire escorts to take her to parties—unless, of course, that appeals to you.

13. Will repeat promises one through twelve until no longer necessary.

The Princess and the Penis

Princesses enjoy sex and try to have it as often as we can, but the difference between princesses and non-princesses is that princesses fill their lives with so much pleasure that sex, though up there, is just one of our daily indulgences. We don't need to talk about sex. We just need to have it. And we don't need Mama Gena to tell us to get in touch with our sexual goddess. We just need the right man at the right time.

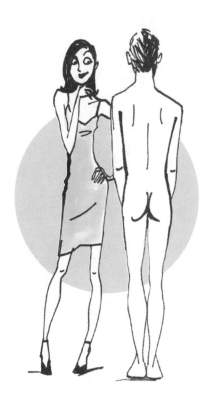

Princess on the Prowl

An informal survey of men (I polled my husband and brother) said that they can sense two women about to have a catfight faster than they can tell it's time for a beer run. That's why it's important for a princess to refuse to embarrass herself in front of would-be lovers. Ladies, it's time to stop sharpening your manicures and sign the Single Princess Noncompete Contract.

SINGLE PRINCESS
NONCOMPETE CONTRACT

I, Single Princess, promise never to . . .

1. Tell mortifying anecdotes about my single friends in front of potential dates—even if the guys aren't that cute.

2. Introduce a friend with embarrassing nicknames, like "This is my friend Chesty, I mean Chessie."

3. Corner her crush after a few drinks and offer tips on how he can get her into bed.

4. Mention her ex-boyfriend or her battle with herpes while making conversation with new, interesting men.

5. Push my way in or push her out of a conversation with single guys, unless she's giving me the eye-rolling save-me signal.

6. Call crush-shotgun by announcing that I have a crush on a guy as soon as we both meet him

so that she can't even entertain the idea of liking him.

7. Ask out a friend's crush when I know how much she likes him and has been waiting for him to call.

8. Conveniently forget to mention that I went out on a date with her crush until a mutual friend spills the beans.

9. Say sexually provocative things so that a guy who seems interested in my friend will like me instead. My penchant for multiple orgasms, the Play-Doh sculpture I made of my breasts, or my last three-way will be banned for cocktail party conversation.

Princess Signature   Date

popular varieties of princess sex
(AND THE MEN WHO PROVIDE IT)

Where you find him	What he's drinking	What's on his feet
The outdoor track at your gym	What's on tap	Tevas
He's a friend of your father's	Eighteen-year-old scotch	Ferragamo loafers
In your phone book	Whatever you've got	Flip-flops
In the bridal party	Champagne	Nothing, he couldn't wait to get out of those one-size-too-small patent leather rentals
The seventh grade. You had crushes on each other then and still enjoy flirting	He stocks your favorite Rioja just in case you call	Clarks

What he's got on underneath	What kind of sex you'll have	In the morning . . .
A Gore-Tex jock	Rugged, outdoor sex: mountains, beaches, tents (even the one you set up in the yard of your parents' country house)	He serves you fresh-brewed coffee at sunrise
Leopard thong	Naughty sex: Why is it that powerful moguls insist on being spanked?	You vow never to tell his wife
Yeah, right	Two A.M. booty call sex: Suddenly you don't need Ambien to help you fall asleep	He's gone. . . Thank heaven
Boxer briefs	Black-tie wedding sex: Half the fun of wearing a merry widow is getting him to unhook it	You blush as soon as you see the bride and groom at the brunch
His lucky underwear	Yummy ego-boosting sex: He's able to make you feel beautiful, divine, and orgasmic— no strings attached	You do it again

Prince Charming vs. the Prince of Darkness

When your knight in shining armor
turns out to be a night in hell.

DATING FOR AMUSEMENT

After a forgettable evening with Dr. No, you can buy yourself a pair of sexy underwear and relish the fact he'll never get to see them. If that doesn't provide enough catharsis, you can always turn your tale of unhappily-ever-after into an amusing story for your friends. For example:

To: princess@yoohoo.com
From: princess@hotmale.com
Subject: Hot sex?

So the other night I went out with this adorable guy—okay, so he was a little bit of a stoner, but I can never resist an Ashton Kutcher look-alike. Anyway, so we go back to my place, and he's all over me, in a good way—and we go into my bedroom. I turn on the bedside light but cover it with the Hermès scarf I was wearing as a bandeau. I undress. He undresses. Things move along rather deliciously. And then I smell smoke. At first I think, "Oh my God he's smoking and making love to me?" I had had three cocktails and no dinner. But then I realize, that can't be. So I open my eyes and see that my gorgeous Hermès scarf has caught on fire and my pillows are also up in flames. So I'm like, the bed is on fire! The bed is on fire! And he whispers, I know, honey, our love is hot. So I yell and say, "No, the bed is on fire!" I then grab the burning pillows and run naked into the bathroom. Throwing water on the bed—and him—putting a damper on everything, to say the least. So I called it a night. And slept in my charred bed alone. He kissed me good night but didn't even offer to pitch in for new linens. Which reminds me, do you have a Chambers catalog?

CALLING ALL CARRIE BRADSHAWS AND BRIDGET JONESES

Now, most princesses can share a good story at their book club, or make their pals laugh all the way to the outlets, but the savviest princesses know that a failed relationship can give you much more than heartache. It can lead to six-figure book deals and television pilots. Are you a "material girl"? If you have done one or more of the following, your next date should be with an agent.

1. You've stopped looking for love. Now you're just looking for laughs.
2. Your date is so lame that, just to get through the appetizer, you've stopped listening to him and have begun to fantasize about a shortlist of stars who could play you in the film adaptation.
3. When a man tells you he thinks he's falling in love with you, your first thought is: This is going to be such a great chapter in my book.
4. You've fastened a mini–tape recorder to your bra.
5. You take a Polaroid and ask him to sign a release statement at the end of the date.
6. You go home, turn on your computer, and type out questions like: Can a princess date a guy who dreams of owning a White Castle?

Manipulation Manuevers

How to get your boyfriend to do what you want without even asking. (Scored on a scale of one to ten.)

Approach: **State an inconvenience**

Technique: Crawl into bed, and say "Oh darn! I forgot a glass of water." Boyfriend should know that's his cue to get out of bed and bring you a fresh glass. (If he doesn't react, repeat. If he still doesn't react, break up with him.)

Success Rate: 10

    Note: The only complaint this does not work for is "I'm hungry." Instead, it backfires and creates a dialogue of "What do you want to eat?" "I don't know, what do you want to eat?" Ad infinitum.

Approach: **Diagnose yourself with a fatal illness**

Technique: Similar to work cop-out, while you're sitting on the couch, you turn to your darling and say in a feeble whisper, "Honey, I'd love to clean up the dishes but my lungs have just filled with a little fluid."

Success Rate: 8

Approach: **News flash**

Technique: E-mail him a late-breaking story. "I just found out the fares to London are only $300 round-trip!"

Success Rate: 6 to 4, depending on how perceptive your boyfriend is.

Approach: **Symbolism**

Technique: If you want him to learn to cook, buy him cooking classes for Valentine's Day. If you want him to give up his sweater-vest habit, buy him some cute shirts to wear.

Success Rate: 5
   Note: Even if he graciously accepts your "gift," he may see right through your scheme and refuse to use the gift certificates or wear the shirts.

Approach: **Sighing/pouting**

Technique: Long, drawn-out sighs are a clear indication to your sweetheart that you want something; unfortunately, it may take him a lifetime to figure out what.

Success Rate: 3 or 10, if you can be patient enough to wait till he clues in.

Wild-Card Approach: **Get him at his weakest**

Technique: When he's hungover, exhausted, hungry, and stressed, mention that you'd really love it if he could finally get you tickets to *La Bohème*, even though he's told you he doesn't like opera. He'll be so tired that he'll say yes just to get you to be quiet. *Warning:* Some princesses have experienced a 50 percent backfire rate where their usually congenial boyfriends have shouted "Stop busting my chops!" and/or "When did you become a professional ball breaker?!"

Success Rate: Use at your own risk.

NEWLY IN LOVE?

If you think it's too early to start manipulating your lover—and it never is—you can ask him to give you what you want directly. But savvy princesses like to use the "Big Buildup" technique to make sure they don't get no for an answer. Before you make your request, lead in with one of the following:

"I have to ask you a *huge* favor . . ."

"I *hate* to ask you this, but . . ."

176   "Oh my God . . ."

For best results, make sure the first two are minor requests, like getting a bowl down from a shelf you can't reach. Then make the third a real doozy, like asking him to attend your second cousin's baby's christening during football season (playoffs). And yes, he'll have to wear a suit.

TIP

To offset disappointment and/or a mistake you may have made: Add, "I have some really terrible news (long pause)," before you tell him what happened. This will make him worry that you have chlamydia, are pregnant, or his dog died. When you tell him that you accidentally left a lipstick in your pants pocket and as a result the laundry (all his clothes) is covered in red streaks, he'll be relieved.

Delegation of Tasks

The happiest princess relationships have open communication, lots of romance, and clearly defined roles.

You	Him
Social director	Bartender
Floral arranger	VCR setter
Nutrition planner	Trash taker-outer
Fashion consultant	Bug remover
Card buyer	Card signer
Call Mother reminder	Fire alarm fixer
Decorator	Ikea furniture carpenter
Housekeeper caller	Vacuum bag installer
Computer complainer	Internet service provider
Gardener	Lawn mower
Takeout/caterer caller	Car warmer-upper
Couch warmer	Snow shoveler
Bed hogger	Ice cube maker
	Fuse box fixer
	Preparty ice getter
	Newspaper retriever
	Wine opener
	Veggie chopper
	Breakfast-in-bed maker
	Foot rubber

Princess Challenge

Remember to love yourself: Call Good Vibrations and order the Natural Contours Vibrator "Magnifique," 1-800-289-8423.

NINE

The Princess Bride

*The biggest party
you'll never remember.*

MYTH:

Princesses are obsessed
with their weddings.

REALITY:

Princesses are obsessed
with their weddings.

Diagnosis: Acute nuptialitis, otherwise known as princess bride syndrome.

Symptoms: Patient suffers from wedding dress obsession. She thinks nothing of lugging two 975-page wedding dress magazines in her purse wherever she goes. Carries fabric swatches, paint chips of the shade of ecru/ivory/linen color she has in mind for her dress. Is more familiar with the names of bridal designers than some of her relatives on the guest list. And she has complained, more than twice, that picking out her dress has been much harder than choosing her fiancé.

Prognosis: Nonfatal, but it can be costly, especially when an indecisive princess bride ends up buying two dresses. Some extreme cases can last for months after she has returned from honeymoon and written all her thank-you notes.

Treatment: Force fluids (preferably champagne) and take the following essay to bed.

SHOPPING FOR a wedding dress is like joining the Peace Corps of Couture—it's the toughest retail you'll ever love. The process is rigorous (back-to-back appointments without lunch), pressured (how many Saturdays can you really spend with your mother?), invasive (septuagenarian seamstresses manhandling your breasts), and unforgettably rewarding (seeing yourself for the first time in "your dress"). But you'll do it, even if you're not a full-time princess, because you're not just buying a dress, you're living out your dream.

Any princess wife will tell you there are five stages of wedding dress shopping. I've suffered mightily through all of them, so hopefully you won't have to.

THE AMBITIOUS PHASE

My mother and I began my search at Saks Fifth Avenue, which offered a healthy selection of celebrity designers and up-and-coming labels. I pulled about ten different dresses ranging from wedding cakes to sexy sheaths. The bridal sales consultant, Vivian, suggested I start with a ball gown by a designer named Amsale. Coincidentally, I had torn out a picture of this dress from a magazine three days before. It was one of my favorites from the stack of pages I had in my bag. The black-and-white ad featured a bride in quiet repose. Engaged only a month, I was already suffering from a recurring nightmare of a tulle tornado that comes to destroy my tiny New York apartment. The Amsale dress had a light blush tint that set it apart from the fleet of shining white and aged-ivory gowns. As Vivian lifted the skirt over my head so I could find my way through the tulle crinolines, I imagined my life as a woman who shopped like this all the time. Vivian buttoned up the back. My mother watched me in the mirror, then covered her mouth and began to cry. The dress was exquisite. The organza was crisp, soft, and weightless. The blush color made my skin glow. Turning to my mother, I heard the romantic swish of the ball gown and I began to cry. We all looked in the mirror and nodded. The dress was perfect. I turned to my mom with tears in my eyes and said, *"Next."*

Princess bride lesson #1: Never buy your first dress. In bridal folklore a mother cries, a daughter cries, a check is written. Not true in the world according to the princess bride. Princess brides see themselves as having two options: They can exorcise all of their tulle and crinoline fantasies by spending the next six to eight weeks searching for *the* dress. Or they can buy the first thing they see and remarry several times to satiate their wedding dress appetite.

THE (DIS)APPOINTMENT PHASE

Snow fell in big light flakes the Saturday we headed up to Vera Wang. It had taken us three weeks to get an appointment. I had a bikini wax and wore my most ingenuelike underwear (blue-and-white lacy bra and panty set) for the occasion. Chauncey, our saleswoman—tanned, in her fifties with a thick torso and skinny calves teetering in Manolos—had me start with the most popular Vera Wang dress: a sheer bodice with a huge tulle skirt that had an endless row of flat bows running down the back. Three years ago my cousin had chosen this dress. Since then, this gown was copied by numerous designers, photographed in every bridal magazine, and featured in teen prom magazines in poor fuchsia-and-green imitations. It had become the entire tristate area's collective wedding fantasy. My mother asked me to try it on "just to see." I indulged her even though I wouldn't know what to do if it was indeed my dress. Unfortunately that wasn't a problem—the dress was awful. The sheer fabric made my arms look like sausages wrapped in tulle, and it cut too high on my neck. I was uncomfortable and annoyed that a dress that had complemented so many figures didn't work on mine. My trip to Vera Wang was turning into Vera Wrong.

Chauncey returned with two more dresses. The first was the dress that Elizabeth Hurley wore in the Estée Lauder Beautiful campaign. I held off, not ready to face another embarrassing comparison. We tried on others, but nothing made us cry. I couldn't help but be disappointed about my appointment at the famous salon. It seemed to be an off year for her. She was quoted as being "pro-color" and set out to break new bridal boundaries with pink, blue, and green ball gowns. Who would test them, I wasn't sure. Young divorcées? Even Chauncey didn't seem to recommend it. Frustrated, I half jokingly suggested the rose pastel. Chauncey shook her head, "Oh no, you'll never want to remember your wedding as the year *we* did pink."

👑 *Princess bride lesson #2:* Get over designer lust. Don't take it personally if the dress or designer you thought would be perfect isn't. Instead, take a deep breath and leave it up to the big wedding planner in the sky and continue to enjoy the attention. Brides who are determined to wear a certain designer dress tend to be upstaged by their gowns. Princesses know the only other person you should share the spotlight with is your own reflection in the disco ball.

The Departure/ Desperate Phase

In week four of the search, Mom and I met at the Madison Avenue store of Yumi Katsura, a Japanese designer I imagined would strike the spare yet celebratory balance I was looking for. But when I came out of the dressing room in a gauzy kimono-inspired dress my mother choked on her glass of Evian. "You look like Florence Nightingale. Take it off," she said, laughing hysterically and dashing all my hopes for a funky Unitarian–Buddhist affair.

👑 *Princess bride lesson #3:* Your wedding should be a fantasy, not a reinvention of yourself.

The Panic Phase

In wedding dress limbo, I began to feel nauseated just looking in bridal windows. While I loved planning the wedding, I was freaked out by my page-long to-do lists that always started with: Find Dress. It was time to buy, time to commit to something, but I was convinced that no one dress could live up to my expectations. I could tell by my mother's chain-smoking and the empty box of Crunch-a-Munch in her car that my indecision was getting on her nerves.

Princess bride lesson #4: Even if you've contacted seamstress nuns in Italy to hand-bead your dress, you will annoy, frustrate, and bore your friends and family by vacillating among all your choices. They may mistake your dress preoccupation for being spoiled and/or crazy. They may even be right. But who cares. Eventually, you will all get over it. This is just one of the reasons you give your bridesmaids and parents thank-you gifts at the rehearsal dinner.

THE POUTY PHASE

On a raw and rainy March day, we went back to Saks and ordered the blush Amsale gown that had made my mother and me cry eight weeks before. My mom was thrilled. I was concerned. The purchase seemed anti-climactic. I tried it on again. Mom and Vivian gushed. The charge was swiped. It was done. Shortly afterward I started to sulk. I'd see other dresses and think, where the hell were you when I was shopping? I questioned the whole significance of the wedding dress and considered changing my black-tie reception to a beach bonfire so I could wear white jeans and a lace bikini top instead. But then I remembered my parents had already sent in the nonrefundable deposit for the reception. When my dad wrote the check he said, "Sweetheart, I want you to know that we support whatever you want to do, but if you back out of this, you better find a girl to get married at the St. Regis on October 11." I resigned myself to the dress and the original plan, but still indulged in self-pitying fantasies, like imagining myself as one of those well-tucked society women who attends so many galas her gown seems like an afterthought. At the wedding, I'd respond to compliments with a wave of my hand, saying, "This old thing."

👑 *Princess bride lesson #5:* You will suffer wedding dress remorse. It can happen even before the ink is dry on the deposit check. As a princess bride you convince yourself you've made a huge mistake and may (a) consider losing your deposit and finding another dress, (b) actually do that, or (c) suck it up and wear it but refuse to get your photographs developed so you won't be reminded of your poor judgment. Wedding dress remorse usually lasts until your first fitting.

THE I-KNEW-IT-ALL-ALONG PHASE

Three weeks before the wedding I was back at the Saks Bridal Salon for my final fitting. Vivian helped me step into the dress. I had forgotten the power of its understatements: the shimmering organza, the way the blush made my skin glow. I looked at myself and I felt so foolish. Why had I second-guessed this? Why had I punished myself, thinking I had made a mistake? What was I trying to prove? All the dresses I tried on were bits and pieces of what I had wanted, but this dress was somehow me entirely. I had known it instinctively. But being a princess bride, and not interested in remarrying in the J. Lo tradition, I had to cycle through all my fantasy weddings to learn that giving myself what I want is really quite simple.

👑 *Princess bride lesson #6:* Trust yourself. You found the perfect man. How could you not find the perfect dress?

what your dress and your fiancé have in common

- You thought they were cute the moment you saw them.

- They've both seen you naked.

- They both make your friends a little jealous.

- You didn't know if they were "the one" until they were on you.

- Your mom thinks you look great together.

- After the wedding they both went to the cleaners.

- They both make you feel like a princess.

The Ring

Princesses see engagement rings as a symbol of a sacred commitment as well as something sparkly to distract clients while we're making a presentation.

Before Engagement Ring	After Engagement Ring

When concentrating...

When angry...

When laughing...

PRINCESS BRIDE MOMENT

Heiress Gloria Guinness could not wear a glove on her right hand because her ring was too big.

Planning

Before you start to plan your wedding or hire a professional planner, set the ground rules of your planning partnership with unpaid friends and family (your mother, sister, or dating coach, who has now been promoted to wedding coach thanks to her great advice) by exchanging the following vows.

• PLANNER TO BRIDE •

I, (insert name here), agree to be your lawfully wedded bridal confidante.

I will cherish your choice of wedding ceremony, hot and cold hors d'oeuvres, and centerpieces today, tomorrow, and forever.

I will trust and honor your ban on the chicken dance, the macarena, and that Celine Dion song from Titanic. *But I'm not backing down on a conga line.*

I will laugh with you when you're trying on ugly dresses and cry with you when we look at the price tags. I will be faithful and go to as many appointments as my schedule permits. I will be there through the good times, when we get buzzed at wine tastings, try on tiaras, and pick out the floral schematic for your cake. And in bad, when we search unsuccessfully for a seamless thong, watch sad, hairy lounge singers pretend to be Harry Connick

Jr., and wait on endless lines to return gifts. And no matter what may come, I will always be there to mention something cute I saw in a bridal magazine. I vow to do all these things till your wedding day do us part. *So help me God.*

• BRIDE **TO BRIDAL CONSULTANT** •

I, (bride), take you, (friend and now planner), to be my law-fully wedded bridal confidante.

I will cherish your opinions and promise not to dismiss your suggestions even though I already have very specific ideas about exactly how I want the flowers, cake topper, song list, and bridesmaid earrings to be.

I will trust and honor you by not acting like a baby (even if I am your baby).

I will laugh with you when we get catering price estimates and cry with you when I find my dress. I will be faithful and share all my wedding plans with you so that on my wedding day you and I will be the only people who notice if the center-pieces are too high, if there are lines at the hot and cold stations, and if, despite our ban, the band still played the macarena (but that you were right about the conga line—it was fun). I vow to do all these things till my wedding day do us part. *So help me God.*

We've all heard horror stories about bitchy brides who push their bridesmaids to the point where they act out by boycotting the bridesmaid dress, yawn during the ceremony, and deliver drunken toasts. But no matter how awful the bride or bridesmaids were, neither is completely to blame.

The problem is that the bride didn't know how to pick a bridesmaid, and the bridesmaid didn't know how to be a friend. Princess brides wait a month (if not more) before they choose their bridesmaids. During that time they carefully consider the emotional, physical, and geographic state of each of their closest friends and screen their candidates with the following questions:

- Does she live near me?

- Is she planning a six-month trip hiking in the Himalayas or having a baby?

- Is she very busy with work?

- Did she just break up with someone?

- Does she have an eating disorder that will be exacerbated by my wedding?

- Does she like weddings?

- Is dusty rose her color?

- Do I even like her?

Once we've completed the initial screening process, we narrow the choice even further: (a) Those who want to get married but aren't engaged. This is ideal for princess brides with friends who've found the china pattern they want, but not the man. (b) Married friends suffering from postnuptial depression (stage three Advanced Princess Bride syndrome, where a married woman would do anything to relive her engagement process). Though this bridesmaid will probably insist you use her florist, it's still a win-win situation. She gets to relive her wedding, and we get a free wedding planner (see Postnuptial Depression, page 205). (c) My mother, Carole Castagnoli, to fill in as a matron of honor (she's listed).

Four Types of Princess Weddings

THE BLOWOUT WEDDING

Tone: Black tie

The place: Castles, country clubs, tents. Hotel bonus: They throw in the honeymoon suite.

The details: Your dog walks down the aisle in top hat and (wagging) tails. Heaters and luxury Porta Potties (for tent weddings), pink lily of the valley flown in from New Zealand for your October wedding, twelve-piece orchestras.

The deciding factor: You wanted to have it at a cool loft, but your mother said that if you did she would insist on decorating the freight elevator in tulle.

The dress: Designer

The ring: Ka-ching

The support staff: Wedding planner (the person, not the notebook) otherwise known as Switzerland. She mediates all major decisions between you and your mother. Incidentally, she unwittingly helps you and Mom bond when you disagree with her suggestions.

Revelation: You realize you're really marrying your mother.

THE BOUTIQUE WEDDING

The tone: Intimate

The place: Thirty of your closest friends fly to Martha's Vineyard.

The details: You insist the pastry chef use organic carrots in the cake (it doesn't matter that you serve it with plastic forks).

The deciding factor: You keep it small because you have too many friends, business colleagues, and/or crazy relatives.

The dress: Custom-made by up-and-coming designer.

The ring: Custom-designed by up-and-coming jewelry designer (cousin of dress designer).

The support staff: Best friend who turns the whole thing into a much bigger deal than you had intended by insisting you wear shoes and register.

Revelation: You secretly love the attention.

THE ELOPEMENT

The tone: Naughty

The place: Las Vegas

The details: You choose the cutest drive-through chapel and secure the honeymoon suite with heart-shaped bed/champagne tub weeks in advance.

The deciding factor: You couldn't agree on the ceremony, flowers, band, photographer, and whose mother to strangle first.

The dress: White jeans and a white Elvis-inspired rabbit jacket.

The ring: You upgraded with your gambling winnings.

The support staff: Elvis impersonator

Revelation: It was your fiancé (not you) who couldn't keep your elopement a secret.

The tone: Highly interactive, awkward for some

The place: You walk down the aisle to the theme from *Star Wars* dressed as Princess Leia and Han Solo at the local planetarium.

The details: You build a *Millennium Falcon* altar and give away action figurines as favors.

The deciding factor: You and your fiancé have an inside joke about his light saber.

The dress: Princess Leia–inspired gown, braids not included.

The ring: Moon rock

The support staff: Fiancé and friends from college who are set designers/producers/lighting technicians.

Revelation: Your mom tries to be supportive by telling you she approves of Dr. Spock's approach to child rearing. You don't have the heart to tell her it's *Mr.* Spock, that he's on "Star Trek," and it's not *that* Spock.

Etiquette—Princess Wedding Do's and Don'ts

Do accept your boyfriend's proposal of marriage, if you really love him, even if the ring isn't exactly what you had in mind. You have a lifetime to upgrade.

Don't tell him that you had imagined something, well, bigger.

Do talk at length to your minister/priest/rabbi regarding the service and whether or not he or she thinks a Hindi commitment ritual is a good idea even though neither of you is Hindu.

Don't fire your minister/priest/rabbi because you think he or she is unattractive and you don't want to see that person in the middle of all your ceremony pictures. He or she is a person of the cloth, not a cover model.

Do keep in mind that your friends have other things beside your wedding on their minds.

Don't ask them to do you special favors such as: only wear strapless bathing suits all summer to avoid tan lines in the bridesmaid dress, join Weight Watchers, or have her baby before your big day.

Do bring photographs or pages from magazines to illustrate the kinds of floral arrangements you'd like.

Don't ask the florist to measure each petal of your orange blossom bouquet to make sure it's perfectly equidistant.

Do have Mom bring Dad along to one of your dress appointments. He is secretly curious (especially if he's paying), and it's a sweet moment you'll always remember.
Don't drop Mom from the wedding dress shopping trip and take your personal trainer because he'll be able to suggest dresses that make you look more buff than beautiful.

Do look forward to your friends' weddings.
Don't spend all your time at a friend's wedding comparing the flowers, food, music, dress, et cetera, to yours.

Warning: If you have more than three don'ts, you are at high risk of becoming a Bridezilla. Friends and family are advised to stage an intervention.

Your Psyche

WEDDING DREAM DICTIONARY

A key to what your nuptial nightmares really mean:

Torn dress: Symbolizes fear of separating from family and friends.

No dress: Fear of commitment.

Blood on dress: Usually connotes worry. The most common worries are: Someone will spill red wine on your dress; you'll get your period the day of the wedding.

Wilted flowers: Sexual incompatibility.

Naked guests: You're afraid your guests won't understand the words *black tie*.

No-shows: Nagging fear that you're getting married on Super Bowl Sunday.

POSTNUPTIAL DEPRESSION

Diagnosis: Princess bride syndrome candidates who enjoyed the wedding planning process so much that they spend the first year of their marriages looking backward instead of forward. This can last a few weeks or the actual length of the engagement. Princesses can catch it from their mothers, mothers can catch it from princesses. Fathers and new husbands are immune.

Symptoms: Princesses will (a) muse, "Oh, I think it was this time last year that we found my shoes," (b) be seen skulking around bridal stores, (c) secretly continue to read bridal magazines and hide her collection under the bed, (d) take a keen interest in friends' weddings, (e) consider a career in wedding planning.

Cure: Time and diversion. See dog, work, or entertaining chapters.

THE WOMEN'S SPORTS PAGES:

Getting Announced in the New York Times

Society pages come and go, but the *New York Times* wedding announcements are forever. Sunday after Sunday, as the wedding announcements expand from three pages to six, it's become clear that it's not really a question of whether your wedding will be announced in the *New York Times* but where your announcement falls on the page.

Princess has devised a simple and precise point system that will help you figure out where you'll be placed and if you pass the *Times's* photo litmus test. Though the *Times* is making an effort to include romantic anecdotes, love does not conquer being a descendant of the D.A.R. The only spread that matters is the first spread. The other pages just go on and on, and rest assured, if you are the ambassador to Uruguay's daughter, your wedding will not be buried on the second spread in the lower-left column.

Please realize that this system is based on June through October only. In fact, one way to assure excellent placement is to get married during the less busy months of January through March, when the paper is desperate for couples. And although no extensive research has been done, this system can be applied to many local newspapers' society columns. Okay, get your pencils ready:

If You or Your Fiancé...	Points
is a member of a now-defunct monarchy, a baron, duke, raja, or count	200 (photo of bride in formal attire)
is special adviser to the president of the United States	100
has spent the last ten weeks on the nonfiction best-sellers list	70
is a doctor or lawyer with celebrity clients	60

If You and Your Fiancé...	
are Chinese violinists	125 (bride and groom in formal attire photo)
are finishing your residencies in pediatric medicine	60 (bride and groom in business attire)
live in D.C., Cambridge, Virginia Beach, or California	50
like to tell people at parties what you do for a living	30

If You...	
are the niece of a Nobel Prize winner	250 (bride and groom in casual attire)
are the great-granddaughter of a founder of Union Pacific or Gulf & Western	150 (bride in formal attire)
are getting a master's in early childhood education	60 (bride in formal attire)
are a magazine editor, PR associate for a fashion designer, or work at an auction house	40

If Your Fiancé . . .   Points

is a descendant of a signer of the Declaration of Independence	200 (bride in formal attire)
is a relatively well-known jazz musician	70 (bride and groom in casual attire)
is a VP at an unscathed financial firm	35

If Your Father . . .

is the brother of the president of the United States	300
was once the ambassador to Pakistan/Zambia/Indonesia and is now a championship polo player/owner of Cleveland Indians/Metropolitan Museum trustee	200 (daughters of ambassadors-turned-trustees wear formal attire, daughters of ambassadors-turned-sports-enthusiasts wear casual attire)

If Your Fiancé's Father . . .

was bureau chief at the *Times/Wall Street Journal*/ABC News	200
is a "vice" something	50

If Your Mother . . .

was Yves Saint Laurent's muse	80
is one of the founders of NOW	79

If Your Fiancé's Mother . . .

teaches movement in New Hampshire	40
belongs to the PTA	0

Sections A and B are the dueling debutantes. They are the best places to be announced outside of the vows column (and for the bride whose family legacy needs no embellishments, the vows seems a bit gauche). Taking its cue from the seating arrangements at a wedding ceremony, if the bride's family is more prominent the wedding will be announced on the left (A). Conversely, if it's the groom who is a distant relative of Alexander Hamilton, the announcement will be on the right (B).

SECTION C, 160–250 POINTS
(center columns—rows one and two)

The second-best spot is section C, which is occupied by well-to-do out-of-towners and New York's power elite. Renowned scientists from Woods Hole, automobile heiresses of Grosse Pointe, and geek millionaires (who got out just in time) from Palo Alto share this space with New York's best anesthesiologists, nieces of cult poetesses, celebrity lawyers, and entertainers. Photos are usually saved for Chinese violinists.

SECTION D, 60 POINTS
(left to right columns, below the fold)

This section is for "below the fold" brides who did not debut. From left to right, the columns are as follows: far left, doctors; second column, lawyers; third column, technology; far right, book publishers, newspaper writers, magazine editors.

The brides in the two columns next to the Vows section were debutantes but unfortunately they suffer from dull jobs the non-debs in section D wouldn't even temp for. It's likely that they attended the same cotillions in high school as the brides in sections A–C but they probably didn't know where the after-parties were.

"Vows" columnist Lois Smith Brady insists that this column isn't about status as much as it is about love stories, and I tend to believe her. But what she lacks in ancestor worship she makes up for in the wacky way opposites attract. Brides are usually described as bubbly with a great backhand, and grooms are known for their fettuccini and rare book collections.

Memorable columns: The Hindu wedding for seven hundred in Upper Brookville, Long Island—the bride's dress was covered in gold and was so heavy she could not stand up. The couple whose wedding was a walking tour of all their favorite places. The Tiffany & Co. sales associate who changed her wedding plans so often she and her fiancé chose to elope, and she wore her unfinished dress by pinning it together with Tiffany's diamond-and-pearl dragonfly brooches. Despite their differences, every wedding Ms. Brady features is a princess wedding.

This section is filled with those nice couples you meet at other people's weddings who are one glass of champagne away from asking you if you could help them get a job at your company.

Perspective

Meditate on the following wedding koan throughout your engagement:

Once there was a bride who painstakingly pressed thirty bars of butter into small hearts. Her wedding day came, she served the heart-shaped butter in cute dishes. Her guests smeared the heart-shaped butter on bread and ate it.

Princess Challenge

*Just because you're married don't believe that
your fairy tale is complete.*

TEN

Are You There, Barneys?

It's Me, Princess

A list of important
names and numbers

your starter kit for fabulousness

- **Your irreplaceable hairstylist who makes weekly house calls:** _____

- **Your indispensable manicurist who makes secret office calls:** _____

- **Your eyebrow sculptor:** _____

- **The best chocolates on earth (so yummy friends don't mind that you forget their birthdays, as long as you send them a box—eventually):** www.lamaisonduchocolat.com

- **That understanding shoemaker who never asks who or what is chewing up your high heels:** _____

- **The best dry cleaner in the United States who will FedEx you your clothes (there and back):** Parkway Custom Drycleaner, 301-652-3377

- **That divine florist who understands your request for a bouquet that's low, bushy, and delicate:** _____

- **The only cleaner you let touch your leather and suede:** _____

- **Your fashion emergency hotline:** _____

- **Ritz-Carlton Hotels:** 1-800-241-3333

- **Prada in Las Vegas** (they always have what you're looking for, even when every other store in the country is sold out): 702-866-6886

- **Custom bra fitter:** _____

- **The best tailor in Hong Kong:**

  Soong
  Han Chung Mansion 8-10
  Hankow Street, Flat A
  852-2723-1400 or 852-2366-0480

- **Your faithful diamond man:** _____

- **Irresistible made-to-measure lingerie in Paris:**

  Alice Cadole
  14 rue Cambon, 1st
  33-1-42-60-94-94

- **Fur storage and closet organizer:**
  Garde Robe, 212-227-7554

- **Your ingenious chandelier washer:** _____

- **That cute champagne delivery guy:**

_____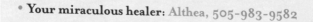

- **That even cuter and terribly discreet bartender-for-hire:** _____

- **Your miraculous healer:** Althea, 505-983-9582

- **The dog whisperer:** _____

- **Your pet detective (God forbid!):**
  Carl Washington, 703-960-9596

- **Barneys Concierge Services:** 212-826-8900, ext. 2466

The energy of imagination, deliberation, and invention,
which fall into a natural rhythm totally one's own,
maintained by innate discipline and a keen sense of pleasure—
these are the ingredients of style.

DIANA VREELAND

Acknowledgments

IT COULD BE SAID that this book was written while shopping at Bergdorf Goodman and having manicures, lymphatic massages, and a few champagne cocktails. I'd especially like to thank the three women who spent so many hours doing princess fieldwork with me: Tanya McKinnon, Ann Shoket, and Sadie Van Gelder. Their friendship, taste, and counsel were invaluable resources that helped shape this book. I'd also very much like to thank my editor, Ann Campbell, who made sure all my princess needs were met and who was steadfast in upholding a princess level of perfectionism even when time was running out; and the entire team at Broadway Books, who never batted an eye at my request for more pink, more pretty, or just more: John Fontana, Jenny Cookson, Terry Karydes, and Natasha Harris. Izak, who understood *Princess* on its most

221

profound levels from the moment we met; Justine and everyone at Traffic, for their diligence and support. Judith Stagnitto Abbate for making it all prettier than I imagined. Sabrina Solin, for her three-hour rule. David Moore, for his love, humor, and for once again taking on the role of human Prozac. Standing ovations, chocolates, and flowers also go out to Kimball Hastings, Laura Forde, Mike Dolan, Nathan Brackett, Edie Meyer, Drew O'Brien, Richard Simon, Dr. Olga Chelselka, and Elizabeth Kuster. A very special thanks to my family: Carole, Bill, and Andre Castagnoli; Connie Savarese, Christine, Tony, and Abbe Moore; Dammon Frecker. And last but not least, Chewie, Princess's best friend.

© Kaija Bereins

FRANCESCA CASTAGNOLI is a senior writer for *Self*. In addition to launching the successful *Princess* 'zine, she has held staff positions at *Harper's Bazaar*, *Cosmo Girl!*, and *Mademoiselle*. She lives in New York City.

IZAK's work frequently appears in advertising for Barneys and Henri Bendel.